AWAKEN

SUSAN K. WEHRLEY

© Copyright 2020 Susan K. Wehrley
All rights reserved

No part of this book may be used or reproduced in any manner whatsoever without the written permission of the author, Susan K. Wehrley, except in the case of brief quotations embodied in critical articles and reviews that are referenced back to "Awaken" by Susan K. Wehrley. All photos used with permission and/or credit given.

Published by Thomas & Kay, LLC

Photography Lisa Wiltz
Editors: Lisa Wiltz and Alex Wehrley
Book Layout: Image 360 New Berlin

Printed by Create Space in the United States

ISBN: 978-0-9729505-5-8

To contact Susan K. Wehrley, for additional coaching and consulting services:
Susan K. Wehrley
Email: Susan@BIZremedies.com
Phone: 1 (414) 581-0449
Website: www.BIZremedies.com

TESTIMONIALS

"The tactical tools and stories, on how to implement and trust my intuition, have helped me gain confidence as a business leader."—Inge Plautz, Vice-President, Old National Bank

"Throughout my years, I have read a lot of books and I have been to many trainings on leadership and human potential. Susan is doing amazing work and has made a difference in my life, both personally and professionally!"—Maria Elena Perez, PHD, LCSW, Vice-President of Behavioral Health

"I loved this book as it took me to the next level in my detachment of my limiting beliefs and helped me recognize and solidify my skills as an intuitive leader." –Dawn Leader, COO, Aegis Corporation

"The book challenged me to be more aware of my thoughts so I can quickly turn my thoughts around into thoughts that serve me vs destroy me!"—Brian Toelle, Founder and Owner, Sell for Millions

"Wow! I will have this one on my desk and out regularly. It not only helps me see and understand how to create a life that is truly for me, but actionable tactics and exercises to be able to do it."—Kim Thiel, Founder and Owner, Your Pet

"Awaken is about seeing the next possibility within you!"—Jenny Schiellack, National Tax Director, PwC

"Susan's explanation of the 5 levels of consciousness and the "how to" process of elevating and maintaining the highest levels of consciousness is excellent!"—Niki Flessas, Owner, Heartlink, LLC

"Very helpful book! The 5 Levels of Consciousness are so clearly laid out, in addition to how to do "The Work" of becoming an Intuitive Leader!"—Micaela Kuntz, CSCP, Director of Sourcing, GMI Solutions

"Awaken is that gentle reminder to follow your instincts, speak your mind, and have the courage to surround yourself with like-minded souls. Live the example and set the standard!"
—Holly Hennessy, Retired and living The Good Life

"I loved the process and guidance of using meditation to "achieve" each level of consciousness and how self-love is vital to achieve the next level. For me that was the most important concept to feeling and knowing: I AM ENOUGH!" –Debra Spina, Owner, Derma Skin Care Clinic

"Awaken is that gentle reminder to follow your instincts, speak your mind, live the example, and set the standard!" –Holly Hennessy, Retired Executive

ACKNOWLEDGEMENTS

A special thanks to my daughter, Lisa Wiltz, who did the photography for the front, back and inside author notes. Not only did she take great photos, she encouraged me on a daily basis with her attention to detail on the cover design and throughout the book. Her continued guidance and support encouraged me greatly! Also, a special thank you to my team of reviewers who also gave fabulous input to help shape the book: Alex Wehrley, Dean M., Maria Perez, Kim Thiel, Dawn Leader, Jenny Schiellack, Deb Spina, Niki Flessas, Brian Toelle, Inge Plautz, Micaela Kuntz, Holly Hennessy, and Mark LaPorte. Thank you all from the bottom of my heart!

A Note from the Author- *Susan K. Wehrley*

The book "Awaken"—came to me intuitively in the summer of 2020, first in visual form, like a movie. While I wasn't planning on writing another book, it was as though I didn't have a choice— the writing just came pouring out of me—as my intuition guided me on each page. Writing never felt so effortless before. Nor have I ever felt like simply a vessel for the words that were being typed on my computer.

As I read the words I was writing, I could see that it was the work I had been doing with my clients over the last 30 years as an Executive Coach. As many of you know, I was mostly a corporate Executive Coach for much of my career, until I sold my big lake house, down-sized, and decided to trademark my Gut Intelligence (GQ) Process. This led me to work with more women executives to help them break through their internal barriers, primarily fear, that kept them from becoming an Intuitive Leader.

While, I'll admit, I originally thought this book was meant to be written for women leaders—the feedback I received from my male reviewers overwhelmingly stated: This book was equally as important and beneficial for men! While brain researchers say that women's brains are wired naturally for intuition, it has been my experience that men can learn these techniques just as easily as women can. Men truly have an advantage in one way: They were conditioned to have the guts to do something about obstacles when they see them. While women may see the cues at tip of the iceberg more quickly; men tend to take a risk and execute more quickly when they see the truth. Both genders have a tendency they need to improve when it comes to Gut Intelligence™ (GQ) and both are very capable of making those improvements! So, while you may sense that there is a slight slant towards helping women leaders in this book, it is for everyone that wants to embrace their intuition and rise to higher levels of consciousness.

Initially, the byline and first chapter of the book was geared towards the "Witch Complex". However, the more I meditated on the feedback I received, the more I realized that men suffered equally from the "Wimp Complex", which also kept them more attached to their ego's desires and, therefore, less intuitively aligned. That revelation is what made me realize that both men and women needed this book so they could awaken to their intuition and potential.

As you will see, the techniques in this book will not only help you to be a better leader, they will help you become more clear, calm, and confident in your whole life. This is especially important in these uncertain times. There has never been a greater time for our struggle with the lower levels of consciousness, and the anxiety and depression, we can often feel as a result of the uncertainty on matters such as: COVID, soaring unemployment, #BlackLivesMatter protesting and the political unrest. As I encouraged my clients to practice these techniques from the book, I heard more and more stories of how their leadership and lives improved amidst this turmoil!

Finally, I want to say that while brain researchers say that women's brains are wired naturally for intuition, it has been my experience that men can learn these techniques just as easily as women can. Men truly have an advantage in one way: They were conditioned to have the guts to do something about obstacles when they see them. While women may see the cues at tip of the iceberg more quickly; men tend to take a risk and execute more quickly when they see the truth. Both genders have a tendency they need to improve when it comes to Gut Intelligence™ (GQ) and both are very capable of making those improvements!

Whether you are a woman or man who wants to become an Intuitive Leader, you will learn in this book that GQ is as important as IQ and EQ. In this tumultuous and ever-changing time, we need GQ more than ever.

This not only requires meditation; it requires the 5 Practices to Elevate your Consciousness and the 15 Characteristics of an Intuitive Leader.

As you practice the skills taught in the book, you will realize that sometimes life gets sticky and you are back in your ego's mindset of fear, judgment and control again. That is because you are experiencing what I call, "The Velcro Effect". The Velcro Effect occurs when something happens and your fear, self-doubt and judgment are now triggered. That's okay—in the book you will learn a very valuable Elevator Meditation that will allow you to re-visit the lower levels of consciousness and do "The Work" to break through any fear that is causing you to react. When you react, it is never what someone else has done or said. It is always because you are not in Intuitive Alignment being open, trusting, and allowing of your intuition to guide you to make effective decisions to achieve your vision, values, and goals. And, if you don't know what your vision, values, and goals are—no worries! You will learn how to create those in the book too!

It is my vision to have every company include this book, and its techniques, in their leadership development programs. Leadership is an inside-out job, and without it, it will be difficult for leaders to navigate these unprecedented times.

Most of all, while on your journey to awaken to your intuition, be sure to be gracious to yourself and others. We are all here to learn that we are deserving enough, capable enough, and loving enough to manifest the life we desire—with the help of our intuition. While some lessons may be easier to apply than others, embrace the journey, as you become more open, trusting, and allowing of your intuition to guide you!

Blessings-

Susan K Wehrley

AWAKEN
THE 5 LEVELS OF CONSCIOUSNESS

Break Free

from Fear

to Become an

Intuitive Leader

SUSAN K. WEHRLEY

CONTENTS

	Acknowledgements	v
1	Break Free	1
2	It's a Matter of Belief	17
3	Elevate Your Experience	39

- Level One: Unconsciousness *(The Basement Experience)*
- Level Two: Self-Doubt and Judgment (The Kitchen Experience)
- Level Three: Self-Awareness (The Closet Experience)
- Level Four: Detachment (The Waiting Room Experience)
- Level Five: Intuitive Alignment (The Rooftop Experience)

4	5 Practices to Elevate Your Consciousness	77

- Be in Nature!
- Pause and Breathe!
- Observe and Meditate!
- Envision!
- Surrender!

5	GQ is the Missing Piece	105
6	"The Work"	119
7	Become an Intuitive Leader	141
	Reference Index	185

Chapter One: Break Free

There is a moment of choice you face when you see or hear something, and it feels off. Will you believe what you are being told; or will you trust that ping in your gut that tells you:
Something is not right!

If you heard this information from an 'authority', you might think you are supposed to automatically believe them and not question—in the name of respect. Maybe you were never told to just believe authority directly, but any backlash you experienced when you questioned them, may have created a sense of discomfort that caused them to kill the messenger. An authority could be a boss if you are an employee; a parent if you are a child; an elder if you are a youngster; a doctor if you are a patient; a priest if you are a parishioner; politician if you are a citizen; the media if you are a loyal viewer to their station; a male if you are a woman; and so on.

Let's admit it—we've all fallen prey to obedience, blind-trust and squelching our intuition and personal power, in some of those situations. But this book is about finding out how to pay attention to when your gut is trying to tell you something, listening to the intuitive voice within, and finding the courage to do something about it. That all transmits from the inside-out: By listening to your ego's chattering voice first, so you can break through its stronghold to discover how it is holding you back. Only then can you awaken to your intuition, that wants to guide you to become your potential.

While this transformation begins by helping you break through your fear, and then awaken to higher levels of consciousness—the ultimate goal is to help you become an Intuitive Leader. Being an Intuitive Leader does not mean you manage other people. It means you manage yourself. When you learn how to break through your own fear to find your intuitive voice, you model that inner alignment to others. This demonstrates to them how to trust in the authority within. Intuitive Leadership means you are aware of what is happening around you and within you so you can make effective decisions to align to your vision, values, and goals—both at work and home. When you learn to do this effortlessly—in a clear, calm, and confident way—you will show others how to lead their lives by your mere example. That is Intuitive Leadership.

Awakening to our intuition requires we give up our 'complexes'. Only then can we become an Intuitive Leader who aligns their decisions to what they love.

Throughout the book we will discuss how the different levels of consciousness effect our personal and professional lives. This includes how fear gets in the way of us having the wisdom to know the truth and the guts to do something about it. This means you will learn how to make decisions based on what you love; not what you fear. While fear is fear, men and women have different complexes that hold them back from awakening to their intuitive potential. These differences are based on our gender societal conditioning.

Women tend to have 'The Witch Complex': a tendency to be afraid of our wisdom to know the truth, and the reluctance to have the guts to do something about it. We fear we will be chastised for our intuition and strength with labels like: 'Witch', 'The Big 'B', 'Aggressive', 'Bossy' and 'Ball-buster'. But when women are playing it nice and acting like Mother Theresa and the Virgin Mary—they are labeled a 'Saint'. This inadvertently tells women to not honor their intuition, and certainty to not have the guts to do something about it.

Men, in contrast, often have a 'The Wimp Complex': a tendency to believe they must be strong in order to be the 'Knight and Shining Armor', who somehow saves the day. While men may not get the 'Witch' label like women do, they have their own negative labels they must deal with when they are too aggressive. They are called labels like:

'Arrogant a—hole', 'Controlling Jerk', 'Bully', and 'Hitler'—all the names we like to call them when we think they are being an egomaniac. And, in addition, when men are not stepping up and being the assertive hero, we expect them to be, who rescues the weak—they get chastised with labels for being passive as well, such as: 'Wimp' and 'Pussy'.

While us women think we have it tough with our labels, men get negative labels when they are being both aggressive and passive. Let's admit it—while these labels are full of judgment, and probably not meant to help us grow when they are said—there might be a grain of truth that calls out our misalignment with our intuition. When you are living in fear of other's validation, and their potential reaction, you lose your connection to your intuition and operate out of your ego instead. This is because you are too focused on pleasing others and controlling the outcome; instead of focused on the intuitive voice within that wants to guide you to create what you truly love.

But when you are Intuitively Aligned, you will sound different when you present your intuitive insights and, likely, will be taken more seriously. A different voice emerges: One that is not aggressive or passive. It is a voice that is full of wisdom, courage, and love. So, in the future, consider labels as a powerful reflection that perhaps you are not listening to your intuition and you are reacting from your ego's fear instead. Other times, it is just someone else's insecurity projected onto you to oppress your truth and courage. When you are Intuitively Aligned, you will know the difference.

As you increase your Gut Intelligence™ (GQ), you will have the wisdom to know the truth and the guts to handle whatever comes your way. Gut Intelligence™ GQ is a decision-making process that includes your gut, heart, head, as well as your intuition. Therefore, it helps you to know the truth and how to speak it in a clear, calm, and confident way—not with a grandiose or insecure demeanor, that is a result of your chattering ego's mind.

Because 'intuition' has often been thought of as a female trait, men have sometimes held themselves back from trusting in this inner intuitive voice. But when I worked with a group of CEO men at a leadership retreat, they all admitted that their best decisions came to them when they stopped trying to analyze it all, let go, relaxed and did activities like: golfing, cutting their lawn, taking a long hot shower, exercising, spending time in nature, and so on. While they didn't refer to this heightened awareness as their intuition—they called it their "gut-knowing." That is why I refer to it as 'Gut Intelligence™ (GQ),' and have trademarked the term and process. But using the term Gut Intelligence™ GQ interchangeably with intuition, we can overcome the gender semantics that make this just 'women's intuition'.

Gut Intelligence™ (GQ) helps you to understand and synthesize the 3 information centers within, along with your intuition, to help you break through your fear so you can make effective decisions. The three information centers are: your gut, heart, and head—all connected by the vagus nerve. Once you learn to break free from your fear and listen to these 3 resources within, you can then surrender to your intuition to help you put the conscious and unconscious pieces of the puzzle together. When you make decisions in this way, you have increased your Gut Intelligence™ (GQ).

The roles of each information center are as follows:

- The **gut's job** is to *alert* you when something feels off.
- The **heart's job** is to *align* you to what it is you want through your emotions.
- The **head's job** is to *assimilate* the unconscious and conscious information so you can make sense of it all.
- **Intuition** occurs when you surrender what your gut, heart and head tell you so you can allow your intuition to synthesize the conscious and unconscious information to give you an "a-ha" knowing—that heightened awareness that tells you what decision is just right for you.

Science tells us that we have more neurons, neurotransmitters, and hormones in our gut, than in our head-brain. [2] So, when you get that gut-alert, and are afraid about a situation, you will automatically send a signal to the emotional center of your brain. This will make you want to go into that fight or flight reaction. When you do that, however, you become the 'Witch', 'Arrogant jerk', or 'Wimp' you do not want to become.

But when you no longer worry about these labels, and instead just focus on increasing your Gut Intelligence™ (GQ), you will be more apt to synthesize the wisdom of your gut, heart, and head. Then, because you are without fear about what others think about you, or expect from you, you will be able to ultimately surrender to the intuitive voice within to guide you.

The more you give your power away to someone else, and the more you fear a potential outcome, the more you are tempted to suppress our intuition.

The Intuitive Leader understands that the gut, heart, and head need to work together, so all 3 internal information centers have a say in decision-making. When we acknowledge the roles of the gut, heart, and head in decision-making, we can let go of the belief that all good decisions are simply 'logical'.[3-5]

We've all had this experience when we didn't trust our Gut Intelligence™ (GQ), put our idea out there as a question, instead of a statement—and hoped for validation. Then, someone squelched our idea and later brought it up as their own idea! Somehow, it's easier to be angry at them for taking our idea, rather than looking at our self and why we didn't trust our intuition. If we're honest, we are really mad at our self for being afraid of taking a risk or for fleeing at the first sound of rejection. If this is the case for you, then it's likely your 'Witch Complex', 'Jerk Complex', or 'Wimp Complex' was at work—suppressing your intuition because of your fear.

Instead of secretly seething inside, and telling everyone else about how you were wronged, look at how your fear kept you from exercising increased Gut Intelligence™ (GQ)! Go ahead get angry! Anger is just an emotion that tells us something needs to change. Ask yourself how you can change by breaking through your fear, so you can trust your intuition to guide you next time—even in the face of initial criticism of your idea. This will allow you to begin to wonder how you can break through your fear so you can become an Intuitive Leader.

It is not others who hold us back. It is our perceived fear of the outcome, and lack of trust in ourselves, that holds us back from being an Intuitive Leader.

Women often blame diversity and inclusion as the root cause that is holding them back from leadership opportunities. However, women often participate in this oppression. We can take our power back and stop being oppressed when we increase our Gut Intelligence™ (GQ) and awaken to our intuition. Only then can we break free from our fear, speak our truth, and embrace our courage within. With increased Gut Intelligence™ (GQ), we can successfully align our decisions to our vision, values, and goals.

While the #MeToo movement just got us started, now is the time to stop suppressing our intuitive ability so we can awaken to the wisdom within and the courage that will help us speak our truth in the moments that matter.

This would include noticing cues at the tip of the iceberg, aligning our decisions to the vision, values and goals—and then using our mind, and intuition, to make the best possible decisions to pivot fast when necessary! We must take ownership of this intuitive gift and break free from our fear—and our need to be validated. Only then can we awaken to our intuition and have the courage to do what is right and best for our self in every moment.

> ***Allowing your intuition to guide you to speak up means you must break free of your fear, trust your ability to see the truth and execute it effectively.***

Realizing this tendency to ignore intuition, because of our attachment to the outcome, is not gender specific. This became clear to me in many of my management meetings when I would see the vice-presidents in a meeting with the C-level executives. When I began my career, over 30 years ago as an Executive Coach, these executives were almost entirely all men. When they were in a meeting led by the CEO, they were often agreeable and careful to not challenge or offend him. I often saw them tiptoeing around his ego, in the hope of their own personal gain.

Then, when I would see these same executives in a staff meeting with their employees, they turned into a different person who was more aggressive: Not hesitating for a moment to speak up, even if it offended their talent. It was obvious to me that they had not yet found their intuitive voice in either case. These same vice-executives were often working late hours: Saying 'yes' to all the demands from the CEO; when they complained to me that they really wanted to say 'no', because their life was out of balance.

No one else can suppress your intuition but you.

Whether you are male or female: You suppress your intuition when you give your power away to someone else because you believe they can make you feel safe, secure, loved and belonging to a group in some way. It is your fear and attachment to the outcome that makes you suppress your intuition. You are not a victim to your circumstances. No one can suppress your intuition unless you give them permission. It's time to break free of all of your fears, so you can embrace your intuition.

In order to break free from your fear, and become an Intuitive Leader, you will have to trust yourself to see the big picture, notice cues at the tip of the iceberg, speak up, gather data to negotiate on your behalf, and express yourself articulately so your ideas makes sense. When you lead at work and at home in this way, you will get noticed because your intuition will not be expressed in a passive or aggressive way. It will be thought through, with an explainable benefit to the vision, values, and goals.

As you begin to work in this intuitive manner, you will sound different. There will not be a sense of fear behind your words, or any behavior that looks controlling. Instead, you will be clear, calm, and confident—even if others label you, don't agree with you, or criticize you.

Trust your intuition both personally and professionally, especially during these uncertain times.

While both men and women have intuition, brain researchers tell us that women are wired for more rapid intuition. This is because they have a corpus callosum in their brain that is more like a four-lane highway—rather than a dirt road. This corpus callosum is key in helping women integrate the wisdom of their gut, heart, and head quickly to improve their Gut Intelligence™ (GQ). [6]

According to the Pew Research Study, while women out rank men, 17 out of 19 leadership characteristics; men have an advantage in having the guts to do something about it. While men may not see the cues at the tip of the iceberg and synthesize the information as quickly as women do; the Pew Research indicates that men tend to be more likely to take risks and execute before women do. [7]

Debra Tannen, gender research specialist, says this her article published in the Harvard Business Review called, *"The Power of Talk: Who Gets Heard and Why"*: [8]

"The CEO of a major corporation told me that he often has to make decisions in five minutes about matters on which others may have worked five months. He said he uses this rule: If the person making the proposal seems confident, the CEO approves it. If not, he says no. "

When we have any fear at all, be it the: 'Witch Complex', fear of looking stupid, being wrong, not being taken seriously, or any other fear—others will sense it. Communication is 7% words, and 93% body language, emotional energy, and tone of voice.[9] When you are feeling fear for any reason, it will send you to the emotional center of your brain, called the amygdala. This is what puts you in a fight or flight reaction. But when you quiet your mind, you will be able to improve your gut-brain axis and reach the executive center of your brain where you have intuition. Because others are intuitive too, they will be able to sense which part of yourself you are operating from and will react or respond accordingly. You will learn more about this in the upcoming chapters.

We've all felt the difference when we intuitively just knew something deep in our gut. We didn't feel the need to be a 'Witch' or an 'Arrogant Jerk' to prove our point. Nor did we flee, like a 'Wimp', at the first sight of criticism. Instead, we stood tall in our intuitive knowing and others sensed our confidence. And if they didn't agree with us initially, we were certain we could catch them up with our intuitive insights, and our quieter confidence.

When we can effectively articulate our intuition, we have broken through our fear and are operating at a high-level of Gut Intelligence™ (GQ). This means we have listened to our gut, heart, and head—quieted our chattering mind—and heard the voice of intuition speak to us before we try to articulate our ideas to others. In contrast, we have all made decisions from only one aspect of our self and have paid the price. For example:

- When you decide *only from your gut*—it often lacks a connection to your vision, values, and goals and, therefore, can seem a bit reactive to others. We see this happen all the time when leaders react to low performance and suddenly announce a "new initiative" of the month!
- When you decide *only from your heart*—it often doesn't make sense later. We see this happen when someone hires someone too quickly, just to fill a position fast. They want the instant gratification of the job filled, but if they skipped steps, like a background check, they may later regret it.
- When you decide *only from your head*—such as the goals that make sense to your C-team, you likely will lack buy-in and support from your talent if they aren't a part of creating the goals.

I'll never forget how my intuition told me that a company I was consulting with needed a teambuilding exercise to strengthen their management team. So, I gave them an assignment to bring an item to the next meeting that represented something about themselves, so they could get to know each other better. I told them that the intention was to create greater rapport and trust.

The leaders were excited to share their hobbies and adventures and brought their fishing poles, pictures of their trips, and so on. Then, one of the managers, who was recently going through a divorce, got in front of the room to show off something he brought. He stood in the front of the room, pulled down his pants and stood there in his bright green briefs. The room went silent. I was waiting for someone to speak up, but no one did.

I'm not going to lie—I had thoughts running through my head like: "Has he lost it?" "Is he trying to get attention, he no longer is getting at home?" Then, when I realized I was in my own internal emotional reaction of judgment, I stopped, breathed-deeply and asked my intuition what to do or say. It was a moment where I knew everyone was shocked and embarrassed.

Then, moments later, I heard my intuition say, "Ask him why he is standing there in his bright green boxers." So, I did. He looked down in embarrassment and pulled up the shorts he intended to show, which he accidently pulled down because he was nervous about public speaking. Now we could all see what he wanted to share: His shorts from Hawaii that had pictures of his favorite places on it! When everyone realized he had made an innocent mistake, they started to laugh until they practically cried.

While for a moment I doubted whether my intuition had led me astray with this activity, the group became so bonded by the experience. The joke became, "What happens in management meetings, stays in management meetings!" Every time the managers saw this leader in the hall, they would say, "How's it going Hawaii?" Years later, they couldn't stop talking about it! And the best part was the team also built rapport and trust that led to better collaborative decision-making.

As you break free from your fear, and take a risk, you allow your intuition to lead. This includes allowing your intuition to guide you in what you need to do and how you need to speak up as things unfold unexpectedly. As a result of awakening to your intuition and trusting it, you will become the effective leader who trusts yourself to do what is needed in the moments that matter.

This might mean you are led to do an initiative, like I was, but suddenly it is not unfolding like you hoped. What will you do? Will you become aggressive and fight to have it go your way? This will make you fall into the 'witch' and 'arrogant' category, as you will be leading from your ego's fear, not your intuition. Or will you flee from the sudden catastrophe and be thought of as a 'wimp' because you were hoping someone else would rescue you? This is also leading from your ego's fear, instead of your intuition.

In the next chapter, you will have the opportunity to understand how your negative belief system causes you to choose fear instead of your intuition. By changing your negative belief, you will be able to let go of your fear that makes you stifle your intuition. By learning how to identify your negative beliefs that drive your fearful behavior, you will become more self-aware and eventually break free from the fear that kept you from being an Intuitive Leader.

Chapter Two: It's a Matter of Belief

The Danish folklore, The Emperor's New Clothes, written by Hans Christian Anderson, helps us to understand how our need to belong makes us squelch our intuition. When we have an authority tell us something is what it is, we often do not want to be the one who challenges them.

> *It's a belief that we are a 'fool' if we go against group think; or, 'authority knows best', that makes us squelch our intuition and play it safe.*

I get it! The story of The Emperor's Clothes reminds me a lot of my own childhood. For years, I was like the minister, official and townspeople who denied their intuition to appease the Emperor and not be labeled, 'a fool'. But, like the child in the folklore, I eventually became the one who told the truth and was scorned for having the intuition that exposed my mother's secret.

In my case, the truth was that the dad, who raised me, was not my biological father. My mom hid the truth from all of us because she had a secret affair with a married man and birthed both my brother and me from him. Whenever I would question her about it, because my intuition kept telling me that the dad that was raising me was not my biological father, she would say, "That's your silly imagination!"

When I was 33 years old, I began to meditate. As a result of my meditation, my intuition told me about a box in the basement that had my dad's blood donor card in it. This revealed that the dad who raised me had a positive blood type, like my mom. This made it impossible for him to be my biological father, since I have a rare blood type: AB Negative. Furthermore, it was such a flux that this box was even in the basement since my dad died when I was 18 years. You can imagine how hard this was for me to approach my mom, after her denial for 33 years.

While I had been afraid for years to trust my intuition and speak my truth, here's what I learned from this experience:

- No one can abandon you, but you.
- You abandon yourself when you don't listen to your intuition.
- When you discover the truth, it usually isn't as bad as you imagined it will be.
- When you speak your truth, it usually isn't as bad as you imagined it to be as well.
- But, even if it the outcomes are as bad as you imagined, your intuition will guide you—and help you to be clear, calm, and confident in handling the resistance and obstacles.

When you get over your belief that your intuition is your 'silly imagination', you feel a sense of connection to yourself that surpasses any other connection or outcome.

Trusting in your intuition gives you a sense of freedom from the entrapments of the outcomes you otherwise would be trying so hard to control. When you detach from manipulating the outcomes, and just speak your truth, you not only feel a sense of connection to yourself, you feel a sense of freedom from fear. When they say, "The truth will set you free," I now understand that that means.

By learning how to effectively trust in your intuition, you build your internal locus of control, instead of giving up your power to others. By focusing on your intuition, as your source for truth and power, you give up your complexes and become more intuitively aligned. This is because 'what we focus on expands.' When you focus on your intuition, instead of other's validation and response, you awaken to who you are, instead of diminishing yourself in order to be accepted.

When you're in unprecedented times, like we are all in—we need intuition more than ever to help us navigate the uncertainty. While logical facts can help us make good decisions, we need to increase our Gut Intelligence™ (GQ) by synthesizing the wisdom of our gut, heart, and head in such a way that we then can open our mind to our intuition.

Steve Jobs recognized the power of intuition when he said, *"Have the courage to follow your heart and intuition They somehow already know what you truly want to become. Everything is secondary."* Of course, we all know that long before Jobs, Scientist Albert Einstein validated intuition too by saying, *"The intuitive mind is a sacred gift, and the rational mind is a faithful servant. We have created a society that honors the servant and forgotten the gift."*

One of my clients, who acquired many businesses, said he relied on his intuition to help him make decisions. He said he would look at the financial statements, but then walk the company and interview the employees. If his intuition told him the culture felt disconnected and uninspired, he would not buy the company, no matter how good the numbers looked. When I asked him how he could assess the culture intuitively, he said, "If people looked up, were smiling, were moving about communicating with each other, and had energy about what they were doing—I knew the business could make money!" He knew the business is its people—its soul.

When we believe that data is more important in decision-making than our intuition, we will resist trusting the intangible facts that add up to the truth.

But, when we believe whole-heartedly that our intuition can put the pieces of the puzzle together for us and guide us in decision-making, we will trust it. Otherwise, hindsight will be '20/20!'

I'll never forget when I took some friends out boating one time on my 20-foot deck boat on Lake Michigan. It was a windy day and I had two girlfriends with me, and a male high school friend I will call 'Bob', to keep him anonymous. Bob wanted to drive my boat. I told him it was rough out there and my deck boat had an inverted "v", quite different to drive than his boat, so I did not feel good about him driving. But he insisted and proceeded to nudge me out of my captain's seat, so he could get in it.

While I listened to my intuition that warned me to not let him drive, and I did speak up, I did not have the guts to stand my ground. Why? We were sparing over the captain's seat, and I already knew it was unusual for a woman to believe she deserved that position on such a big lake, under such windy conditions. I was wavering, and he could sense my lack of confidence.

> ***When we believe we do not deserve a position of power, others will sense our fear and not follow us. This becomes a self-fulfilling prophecy.***

Well, just as I suspected, he started to drive too fast and was crashing into the waves. I asked him to slow down, and he dismissed my request, telling me, "I've got this!" Then, one wave came barreling over the front of the boat and caused my two girlfriends in the boat to fall onto the floor. One of them fell to her knees so hard, her knee started to bleed!

When this happened, I told Bob to get out of the captain's seat, I was taking over for the rest of the trip. Interestingly, one of my girlfriends went to his defense and said to me, "Susan, you are so strong—no wonder guys have a tough time with you!" I could not believe it. Really? We were going to focus on how I was strong and that was a problem; verses focusing on how my male friend dismissed me and wasn't very intuitive! While we all must keep in check how we speak our truth, I was clear that I had said it in a clear, calm, and confident way.

I knew intuitively what was going on: We were up against a belief that women should not be so strong as to challenge a man and take over the 'captain's seat'. Our conversation on the way back in the boat was quite enlightening, as I challenged everyone's thinking and beliefs about women's intuition and strength. This included how women are held to a different standard than men when it comes to speaking up and taking a position of power. This makes it difficult for women to express their intuition and challenge men when they fear they may offend or be judged.

Men face negative beliefs too that keep them from listening to their intuition. As mentioned before, men have the 'Knight and Shining Armor Complex'—believing that if women are at all wavering—they should step in and rescue. They were raised to believe that their job is to provide and protect. But, when they step in, without the guidance of their intuition or our permission, we call them a 'controlling jerk', like I did with Bob (not outwardly, but in my head, if I'm honest). After much discussion, Bob admitted that he sensed my fear and felt he needed to step in, because I impishly said I did not want him to drive.

We all have these 'learned' beliefs that give us a gut-alert when the script is unraveling in front of our eyes. It's as though we know our part in a movie and, therefore, we automatically take our roles. For women, it's the weak 'Damsel in Distress'. And for the man, it's the 'Knight and Shining Armor' that saves the day. Neither of these roles comes from the guidance of our intuition, as both are societal norms we've been conditioned to follow. While these roles are changing, we still struggle to release our beliefs and the automatic behaviors that follow.

When we begin to look honestly within our self for these unconscious beliefs that drive our behavior, we will begin to understand why we are getting the results we are getting.

While we often say we want something other than we get, we don't realize: We are being driven by an unconscious belief that tells us: We are 'not enough'.

This is our primary negative belief that can be broken down into three specific aspects:

- I am not deserving enough
- I am not capable enough
- I am not lovable enough

Feeling not deserving, capable, and lovable enough can adversely affect you as a leader. If you are operating out of your insecurity, you will make decisions to try to fill your own 'insecurity bucket'. This contrasts to making the hard decisions that your intuition may be asking you to make to effectively align to the vision, values, and goals. While you may think that you are taking care of yourself by making decisions that soothe your fear, you are ultimately missing out on the best possibility your intuition could provide. In addition, abandoning yourself, and your goals in this way, will eventually affect your confidence.

To be effective, we must be a Norton Virus Scanner to our self: Removing the bugs in our programming that disrupt our ability to trust our Intuitive Inner Voice.

By removing the unconscious negative beliefs, you have stored in your unconscious mind, you can re-write the beliefs and awaken to your intuition. Your negative beliefs root back to your childhood. When you explore what happened to you from birth to eight years old, you will find the root cause.

As you begin to realize your belief, 'That you are not enough', you can start to transform the root cause that held you back.

I call this 'The Velcro-Effect'. The Velcro Effect occurs when we have an unconscious belief about our self that makes for a sticky situation. Instead of looking at the belief within us that is holding us back, we tend to point our finger at others for holding us back. If we are going to move forward and become our potential, we need to closely examine our unconscious beliefs that are getting in the way of us listening and executing our intuition's guidance.

I remember a time when I was a consultant for a construction company. I would attend management meetings where we strategized on best practices to meet the goals. After several meetings, I had a sense that the top salesperson did not have his head in the game. There were little things that were adding up: No one knew where he was most of the time, he was not putting information in the CRM, and he wasn't taking team members out on calls, etc.

When I talked to the president of the company about why this salesperson was not being held accountable for these best practices, I learned that the salesman had 65% of the company's book of business. I told the President that it is never good to have someone have this much stake in the company's sales, whether that was a salesperson or a client. I also told the president that my gut was telling me that this salesperson was on his way out to start his own business—and with that much success, why wouldn't he? The president at first was defensive and angry with me. Why? Because my intuition was shedding light on something he did not want to see, hear, or deal with. It was easier to scapegoat me than it was to face his fear of the unknown before he figured out what to do.

In this example, I could stand strong and not wobble, even when the President said to me, "You don't know what you are talking about!" Instead of flinching, I raised an eyebrow, nodded my head up and down, and empathetically said to him, "Unfortunately, I think I do." By standing in the confidence of my intuition, with empathy for his resistance, the President began to re-track his statement, by saying, "Well, okay…I'll look into it!"

> **We detach and let go of our belief that we are 'not enough', when we can focus on that which we intend to create.**

While I was aware that the president had the power to let me go, I stayed focused on my vision: To make him a better president and to help his company grow. As I focused on my positive intention and my intuitive knowing, any fear I otherwise would have about my job security faded away. I knew that once he got over his defensive reaction, he would look into what I said. My goal was not to be liked by him, or to make him comfortable. My goal was to make him and his company successful. While he may have felt challenged by me in the process, I knew that one day he would thank me.

As it turned out, the president called a few of the salesperson's accounts that he knew. And yes, the salesperson had been mentioning to them that he was considering opening a new business. So, my client contacted his attorney, locked the salesperson out of the CRM, showed him to the door and immediately contacted the rest of the salesperson's accounts, so he could build rapport and trust with them. This saved the company from losing any business. And yes, he eventually thanked me for having the wisdom to know the truth and the guts to speak up about it. In this case, because I did not waver in my confidence regarding my intuition, I was able to get the president to trust in my intuition and take action.

Success is first an inside-out job. The inside-out job always begins with you!

To be a successful Intuitive Leader, you must not carry around any unconscious belief that tells you that you are not capable enough to challenge authorities, like the president of a company! You also must trust in yourself, your intuition, and know that you are capable enough to speak your truth in an effective way! If you are always doubting yourself on your capabilities, your fear will keep you from hearing your intuition.

For me, finding my confidence at work, is not as difficult as it is for me to find my confidence in my romantic relationships. Like all of us, our beliefs begin to get formed when we are birth to eight years old. When I was growing up, the dad that raised me used to affirm me my capabilities by saying to me, "You could be the president of anything if you wanted to be!" He first said that to me when I was running for student council president and I gave him my speech. He didn't criticize it, but instead affirmed me.

My mother was great at affirming my capabilities too. I remember that she used to do her food brokerage business from our kitchen table. I would sometimes hear her on the phone trying to close a deal. When she didn't close the deal, I would tell her what I thought she could've done better. Instead of getting defensive, she would affirm my intuition and say, "Wow, that was brilliant! I will do exactly what you suggested next time!" Keep in mind I was only 16 years old, so I had no business experience or education in business at that age, so her affirmation really helped me to trust my intuition when it came to coaching people.

As a result of my parent's affirmation towards my capabilities, I have a belief that I am capable. This helps me to trust my intuition when it comes to work situations, even when I am challenged. When I am challenged, there is nothing for someone's criticism to Velcro to, because there is no negative belief inside of me that tells me, "I am not capable". This doesn't mean I always think I am right. It just means that I don't take it personally, and get defensive, when I am challenged at work. Instead, I continue to take risks and simply get curious when someone disagrees with me, because I do not fear rejection or fear that I am enough.

However, when it came to romantic relationships with men, I had to work on healing the belief that I was not able to trust myself and that I was someone who deserved to be loved. This is because my mother denied the truth of my birthfather and my intuition. She also tried to control who I dated and married and, therefore, did not honor my intuition. This caused me to doubt myself for years, because my intuition told me what I wanted was quite different than what my mom told me I 'should' look for in a man.

While these negative beliefs stem from our early childhood, they affect us as leaders. If we are unconsciously feeling like we are not enough, we will try to fill our empty bucket to self-satisfy, instead of doing what is right and best for the company. The key is to find out which negative belief is more dominant for you and the storyline that made you believe you that you are not deserving, lovable or capable enough.

Once you can identify the negative belief and storyline, you can re-write your story and change your belief. It's funny how it all works: When we are ready to awaken the unconscious belief and re-write our story, our 'teacher' appears. This could be a person or a situation in life that shows us what we need to know so we can let go of our old negative beliefs and replace them with a new one. I had two "teachers" back-to-back, that helped me heal my negative belief that I was not enough.

The first 'teacher' healed my father wound. His name was George Dalton, the founder, and former CEO of Fiserv. George and I were on a Board of Directors together. One day George asked me a question, "If you could change anything in your industry, what would it be?" I told him my idea and he thought it was brilliant, so he said, "Let's do it together!" So, we began our business venture—only to find out weeks later that George had to get four bypass heart surgeries. George decided to do all four at once and unfortunately ended up in the ICU for 7 months. Most of his children were out of town, so I helped his wife by visiting George 3 times a week in the hospital. As I sat by his bed, I often wiped his forehead, fed him ice chips, and talked to him about business—which he said was his favorite topic.

After 7 months in ICU, unfortunately, they said that George was ready to die. But George had a hard time letting go and hung on for weeks. The last couple of weeks, his family decided to have no other visitors besides immediate family. Then, one day I got a call from his wife. She told me that she thought George was having a hard time letting go because he needed to say good-bye to me and that he needed to be reassured I would be okay. So, I went in to see him. I held his hand and wiped his forehead one more time as I reassured him, "I'd be okay, and it was okay if he had to go."

Then, I told George how much he meant to me, and in an odd way, how he had been like a dad to me. George knew that I had lost my dad from a heart attack when I was only 18 years old, so I think he took an extra liking to me, in a fatherly sort of way. But I never really told him how he filled that space in my heart. So, I took this moment to do so. Not knowing if he could hear me or not, I asked him to give me a sign. He winked at me and gave my hand a little squeeze. I started to cry. That night, just hours later, George died peacefully.

There was something about George that was a beautiful combination of my birthfather and the dad that raised me. My birthfather was an intelligent and intuitive entrepreneur like George; and the dad that raised me had a big heart and was affirming like George. It wasn't until the night that George died, that I realized I had been carrying around with me an unconscious belief that I wasn't lovable enough. This was because my birthfather never knew me while I was growing up; and the dad that raised me died suddenly of a heart attack, only weeks after I went away to college. At some unconscious level, it felt like both had left me because I wasn't lovable enough. But that night, when George needed to see me before he died, I realized I was lovable! I was able to see that the prior circumstances of my life had nothing to do with me or my worth.

Having this healing experience with George led me to make more loving choices for myself that were led by my intuition. This set the tone for what I then expected in all my relationships, personally and professionally. The years to follow, I found myself stepping into the power of my intuition in a different way because I believed I was not only capable enough—I was also lovable enough to be supported.

If people were offended by what I was saying, for example, I didn't think their reaction meant I was unlovable or not capable of communicating well. I now knew their reaction wasn't personal and, therefore, I could empathetically encourage them to be more open to feedback and to collaborate to improve results. This change in my belief system, changed me from the inside out—positively transforming how I treated myself and others.

This then led me to my second 'teacher'—a man I met at an international conference where I was the keynote speaker. This relationship healed my mother wound. When I met him at the conference door, as I greeted the guests before I spoke, I got a chill down my body as I heard my intuition tell me, "This is your person!" Just as we were about to shake hands, and before I got his name, the conference coordinators grabbed me to mic me.

Two weeks later, he emailed me and said he wanted to hire me as a consultant for a business he owned. I did not know it was the same man at the door. So, we agreed on a contract and a couple weeks later I was on a plane to meet him at his business, which was in a different country. When I arrived at his business, the elevator doors opened—and there he was, standing to greet me.

Long story short: I ended up being his consultant for several years, flying back and forth to his country, mostly every other week. During that time, we really got to know each other. But, while he expressed interest in me, and I was equally as fond of him too, I chose to not get romantically involved. This was because it did not align with my business ethics, nor did I want to move to another country. In addition, he had not officially broken up with his long-term girlfriend before he began speaking to me about how a long-distance relationship could work with him. This reminded me of how my birthfather must have reeled in my mother while he was still married. By being able to open my heart; yet allow my intuition to guide me—I realized I am capable of making wise decisions for myself in the area of love, unlike I believed my mother was capable of doing.

Often, we believe that our intuition is leading us down a path to a certain outcome. When you don't get the outcome you perceived, look more deeply for the purpose.

What's your belief and story that is holding you back from completely trusting yourself and your intuition? When we heal the root cause to our negative belief—that we are either not deserving, capable or lovable enough—we awaken to our self and intuition. If you want to change the results in your life, work backwards to discover your unconscious beliefs that drive your thoughts, feelings, behavior, and results in your life.

While these unconscious negative beliefs, of not being enough, may seem to have personal implications, they also have professional ones as well. While we often separate our personal and professional lives in our minds—we are who we are! Therefore, these unconscious negative beliefs affect us not only in our personal lives, they affect us professionally too.

On the next page, you will see an illustration on how this works, by viewing The Self-Fulfilling Prophecy diagram. You will also come to understand how believing you are not deserving, capable or lovable enough will affect your ability to be an Intuitive Leader.

Self-Fulfilling Prophecy

Beliefs:
Your unconscious operating system that tells you if you are enough or deserving of what you want

Thoughts:
What you tell yourself about your situation and your ability to get what you want

Feelings:
Your emotions, caused by a result of your beliefs and thoughts

Behavior:
Your actions you take based on what you believe you can achieve and how you think and feel as a result

Results: Your self-fulfilling prophecy!

It's all a matter of belief. And beliefs create one of two mindsets—

- Fear, Judgment and Control
- Open, Trusting and Allowing

Living from the mindset of fear, judgment and control will automatically send you into a lower level of consciousness that triggers the emotional center. The amygdala is activated when you get a gut-alert that triggers an unconscious belief that tells you, "I am not capable enough to handle this situation!" or, "I am not lovable enough for others to support me in my efforts!" When that belief and thought is triggered, you will automatically go into one of these two unconscious reaction patterns:

- Fight (Striving and driving to control the outcome)
- Flight (Withdrawing your efforts and shutting down)

In the upcoming chapters, you will have a chance to do several exercises to help you become aware of your tendency to not feel enough. This could be that you don't feel that you are:

- Deserving enough.
- Capable enough.
- Lovable enough.

When that negative belief gets triggered in you, you will also have an opportunity to wonder what your reaction tendency is. Is it to go into a:

- Fight reaction?
- Flight reaction?

In addition, later on you will learn a meditation that will help you pinpoint when these unconscious negative beliefs were formed—usually from birth to eight years old. Be sure to do The Elevator Meditation, later in the book, to find your unconscious belief.

Keep in mind: It is the negative belief in you that is keeping you from trusting your intuition, and, therefore, getting what you want. It is not your circumstances—no matter how tumultuous they may be. You are not getting what you want because of a negative belief system in you that tells you—that is what you deserve because you are not enough.

As you let go of your old fearful and limited beliefs and thoughts that are holding you back—the truth will set you free to make choices that honor your intuition and power. This means you will transcend all your fearful beliefs and thoughts and replace them with the knowledge that you are deserving, capable and lovable enough, to get what you want. As a result, you will become an Intuitive Leader who can make effective decisions in both your personal and professional life.

In the next chapter, you will learn how to elevate your consciousness so you can break free from your negative beliefs, awaken to your intuition, and listen to its guidance in each moment.

Chapter Three: Elevate your Experience

When we listen to the content of most conversations, especially the controversial ones—we realize the level of consciousness most people experience. This consciousness is one of: Fear, judgment, and control. There is so much polarization on these important issues, it can cause much anxiety and depression.

Can you imagine how we could better resolve these concerns if people were more open, trusting and allowing their intuition to show them, 'The Grey Matter'? The Grey Matter is that place of resolution where it is not 'this or that', 'all or nothing' or 'black and white'. It is a place of 'AND': *"How might I have 'this AND that'?"* By tapping into your intuition, you can elevate your experience and find the place of 'AND' to help you resolve polarization. When you surrender your need to be right, and in control, you can open yourself up to possibilities—and find The Grey Matter, with the guidance of your intuition.

When someone is coming from their intuition, instead of their ego, their response to differences is different. They can agree to disagree and continue to be curious, instead of going into judgment. When we are more open-minded, we can surrender to our intuition and trust and allow it to show us how different opinions can actually lead us to The Grey Matter—a possibility that considers 'this and that'.

Unfortunately, what most of us have not learned is how to elevate our experience during tumultuous times. During unprecedented times such as this, we tend to lock down into the corners of our mind where we get a sense of safety from our own righteousness and identification with a group. In these uncertain times, we crave certainty. It's as though a switch gets flipped in our brains and suddenly, we are in a 'fight' or 'flight" mode, trying to be right and in control because we unconsciously feel so out of control.

You know when you are in 'fight' mode, because you have a chattering mind that tells you, "If it's meant to be, it's up to me!" This leads you to the grandiose and arrogant side of your ego, that edges your greatest self out—your intuition. Your tendency is to take control because you think you are right! When you are in a 'flight' mode, it is because you have lost your voice and sense of power. This causes you to leave the conversation or situation, at least for the moment. You leave as a way of being in control, as you secretly believe you are right. In both the 'fight" and 'flight' experiences, you are in your ego. As a result, you are unconscious of your reactions and full of self-doubt and judgment. This contrasts with being connected to your intuition that allows you to have the ability to be in 'The Grey Matter', so you can see possibilities you otherwise couldn't see.

The census bureau's recent report indicates a third of Americans show signs of clinical depression and anxiety. Maurizio Fava, MD, psychiatrist-in-chief, at the Department of Psychiatry at Massachusetts General Hospital, said this, "It's quite understandable the COVID-19 pandemic is likely to cause significant stress and psychological distress for a large proportion of the population. We know the rates are progressively increasing."[10] The various factors that contribute to our anxiety and depression, include: Trauma from widespread disease, grief over losses of life, fear of getting sick, unprecedented physical distancing, loss of community, financial and unemployment concerns, reduced access to caregivers, and political and economic uncertainty.

When we elevate our consciousness, however, we can let go of our fears and detach from the mass consciousness around these events. To elevate your consciousness, you will learn about 'The 5 Levels of Consciousness'. When you realize how your thoughts are creating your experience, you can change your thoughts and, therefore, elevate your experience.

The 5 Levels of Consciousness will teach you how you can elevate yourself, and your experience, even in these tumultuous times. You do not arrive at a level of consciousness. Your level of consciousness can change according to what aspect of your life you are dealing with or with whom. You will be at higher levels of consciousness when you are detached from the outcome and freer to be present with yourself and intuition. Where you are more attached and in a mindset of fear, judgment, and control—you will struggle in the lower levels of consciousness.

You will learn in this chapter, and the upcoming chapters, how to become more Intuitively Aligned in all aspects of your life—as that is the ultimate goal. As you become more Intuitively Aligned, you will become a leader who has broken free from their fear and can lead from their truth and power.

5 Levels of Consciousness

Level Five: Intuitive Alignment

Level Four: Detachment

Level Three: Self-Awareness

Level Two: Self-Doubt & Judgment

Level One: Unconsciousness

The Five Levels of Consciousness

- **Level One: Unconsciousness:**
In this level of consciousness, you experience anxiety and depression. This is because you are focusing on what is happening, instead of what you can do about it. In this level of consciousness, you are likely using distractions and addictions, instead of dealing with what is bothering you internally. To elevate your consciousness, focus on what is happening internally and what you can do about your external issues. It is also helpful to not view so much negative news and instead to spend more time in nature. Nature has a way of calming us and bringing us back to our center. Exercising in nature, like a brisk walk or bike ride, can additionally stimulate your intuition, as it will help to send the neurons, neurotransmitters and hormones up the vagus nerve to get processed in your gut, heart and head.
- **Level Two: Self-Doubt and Judgment**:
In this level of consciousness, you are recognizing your chattering mind more and realizing how it is filled with self-doubt and judgmental thoughts. While this is not comfortable, at least you are moving away from distractions and addictions and noticing your self-doubt and judgment. As a result, you are becoming more conscious of how your self-doubt and judgment is creating your feelings of anxiety and depression, not your circumstances. To slow down your chattering mind, pause and breathe more deeply into your gut. This will also ease your anxiety and depression.
- **Level Three: Self-Awareness:**
At this level of consciousness, you are becoming aware of yourself and how you want to go into a fight or flight reaction when you feel anxious and depressed. While you became more aware of your thoughts in level two, you are now becoming more aware of how these thoughts and feelings created a fight or flight reaction in you. Now, you are also beginning to have a

sense of wonder about your negative belief that is driving your thoughts, feelings, and reactive behaviors. As you observe your tendency to believe you are not enough to handle your situation, you begin to neutralize your emotions and sometimes catch yourself before you react. As you practice observing your reactive tendency, and meditate at least 20-minutes a day, you will create a better gut-brain axis. This will help you to function out of the executive center of your brain, instead of the emotional center called the amygdala.

- **Level Four: Detachment:**
At this level of consciousness, you are beginning to break through your tendencies toward anxiety and depression and the fight and flight behaviors that follow. You are also detaching from the old negative beliefs, that tell you that you are not enough. These are the negative beliefs that used to drive your thoughts, feelings, behaviors, and results in your life—which you are now detaching from. This is because you are now operating from the executive center of your brain and focusing on who you are and what you want to create; verses what might happen to you and the fear that it produces. By focusing on what you want to create: Your vision, values, and goals—you increase your locus of control and feel more empowered.

- **Level Five: Intuitive Alignment:**
When you let go of your fear, create a plan, and surrender to something bigger than yourself—you become more clear, calm, and confident no matter what circumstances you are facing. At the 5th level of consciousness, you are rising above your circumstances and surrendering your cares to your intuition with a "How might I...?" problem-solving question. By surrendering your cares and questions to your intuition, you change your mindset to one that is more open, trusting, and allowing of your intuition to guide you. As a result of this regular practice, you begin to change your belief system and realize you are enough:

No matter what happens, you will figure out what you need to do, even in the most tumultuous times.

In John 14: 16-17 of the Bible, Jesus talks to His disciples and says, "And I will ask the Father, and he will give you another advocate to help you and be with you forever—the Spirit of Truth—you know him, for he lives with you and will be in you."

In addition to this Bible reference, brain researchers tell us that our ability to provide rapid, accurate answers engages a small area in the brain's basal ganglia, a hub for executive learning, habits, and automatic behaviors. Ultimately these structures link back to the cortex, creating a series of cortical-basil ganglia loops of rapid information we call intuition.[11]

We have all had this intuitive experience where a solution just appears out of nowhere. For example, an executive can be looking at a spreadsheet and in seconds know something isn't quite right.

When you elevate your consciousness, you elevate your experience, no matter what your circumstances might be.

To help you elevate your experience and awaken to your intuition, let's go through each level of consciousness in more detail by imagining you are an elevator operator. Imagine you have 5 floors of consciousness to choose from, each on a separate floor. As you walk into the elevator, you get to press the button and corresponding floor of consciousness you want to choose. It's okay to choose whatever floor you want to be on—you are the elevator operator and the co-creator of your life.

By choosing which floor of consciousness you want to be on, in every moment, you choose your experience in your life. This requires noticing when your ego is in control, in the lower levels of consciousness. When you choose the higher levels of consciousness, you will notice your intuition is guiding you and helping you manifest what you want, by creating synchronicity. The goal is to simply observe the ego when it appears, bless it, and thank it for trying to protect you. The ego is that aspect of you that learned what would make you safe, secure, loved and belonging to a group. These were the beliefs others had for you that you absorbed.

So, to illustrate in more detail, let's take a tour of each floor of consciousness, as though we are visiting them from the elevator. Let's start from the bottom floor to the top floor of consciousness, so we can visit each level and get you familiarized with what is on each floor.

Remember: You are the elevator operator and get to choose which level of consciousness you want to be at in every given time. This is your free will. Intuition never comes barging in on you. You must choose that level of consciousness for it to speak to you and guide you.

In each level of consciousness, outlined in the upcoming pages, you will learn:

- Your **beliefs** that are driving your thoughts, feelings, behavior and results in your life.

- How your **gut, heart and head** are operating and how that is affecting your Gut Intelligence™ (GQ).
- Your **defense mechanisms** and how they are keeping you from higher levels of consciousness.
- Your ability to **manifest** the life you want and why.
- The **thoughts** you have as a result of your beliefs.
- The **feelings** you have as a result of your thoughts.
- The **behavior** you have as a result of your feelings.
- The **results** you have as a result of your behavior.
- The **steps** to take to get to the next level of consciousness.

The Five Levels of Consciousness:

Level One: Unconsciousness *(The Basement Experience)*

Level one consciousness is based on the ego's pride and shame. In this level of consciousness, you want to be in control and independent of your intuition, therefore, you are unconscious of your intuition's promptings.

The two primary **beliefs** that are hallmarks of the ego are:

- Prideful ego: "If it's meant to be, it's up to me"
- Shameful ego: "I am not enough, therefore, why bother!"

As you can see, in this level of unconsciousness, one often flips back and forth from both sides of the ego:

- Grandiosity: Striving and driving to be enough (Fight mode to be enough)
- Self-doubt: Feeling like you are not enough (Fleeing from the challenge)

While it may appear that the person with the grandiose ego is confident; grandiosity is a mask for insecurity and an overcompensation of one's unconscious fear. Conversely, self-doubt is an underestimate of one's capability because they are not acknowledging the help from their intuitive guidance.

In this level of consciousness your gut, heart and head are not in synch. Your gut is in control, and, instead of alerting you to what it is going on, it is sending a warning signal to the emotional center of your brain (the amygdala). This signal is telling you that you have only two choices: Fight or Flight. At level one consciousness, you are operating at the lowest level of Gut Intelligence™ (GQ) because you are very reactive to situations and are unconscious to why you are reactive: You are reactive because you are looking outside of yourself for safety, security, love and belonging.

While you don't understand this yet: You are reactive because unconsciously you believe you are not enough to handle what is going on. This causes you to focus externally, instead of internally to discover what is possible, with the help of your intuition.

You are also unconscious about what your choices are to improve that belief that is driving you unconsciously to create limitation in your life.

Here is what is going on, more specifically in your 3 'brains', all which you are unconscious to you. As a result, you are operating at the lowest level of Gut Intelligence™ (GQ):

- **Gut**:
  Our relationship with self begins in the gut. Do you trust yourself and that gut-alert that says, "It's time to pay attention! Something is not going as you hoped or is not congruent and adding up!" In this lower level one unconsciousness, Basement Dwellers don't get a ping in their gut—they get a punch in their gut that sends them into the amygdala (emotional center) part

of their brain. This creates a reaction, instead of an effective response to situations! It's as though the gut-brain is turned up at full volume as a protection center, and therefore, this creates a lot of emotional reaction and drama. This is because, at this level of consciousness, the gut-brain axis is not yet developed. Without this connection to the heart and head, the gut becomes an impulsive center, not an alert-center, as it was intended to be. In this lower level of unconsciousness, all decisions are: 'Black and white', 'all or nothing', 'either/or', 'fight or flight' decisions. Instant gratification, not long-term results, is the focus. Your gut is leading now and causing you to react.

In this level of consciousness, you will be prey to either distraction, disease, or addiction. Distractions, disease, and addictions can range from:
- Co-dependent relationships
- People-pleasing
- Avoidance
- Busyness
- Perfectionism
- Over-performance
- Drama: Caused by reactions of fight and flight
- Physical diseases: Anxiety, depression, heart attack, cancer, etc.
- Addictions: alcohol, food, drugs, shopping, workaholism, etc.

- **Heart:**
At this level of consciousness, you are not aware of what you desire. That means you do not have a vision, values, and goals for your life. As a result, you go through the motions, instead of setting your intentions. But, while you do have expectations, you are unconscious of what they are because you are focused on your 'not goals'—your fears. Overall, you are numb to most of your emotions.

- **Head:**
Instead of thinking about possibilities, the Basement Dweller spends their time thinking about what defense mechanisms will work to protect them, should their fears they imagine come true. They are using their mind to play defense, not offense in their life.

    The most popular **defense mechanisms** are:
    - ***Switch and blame:*** Unconsciously avoiding accountability and reflection of oneself by finding something or someone to blame.
    - ***Denial:*** Unconsciously failing to acknowledge a truth that may feel unacceptable.
    - ***Projection:*** The unconscious transfer of one's own desires or emotions to another person.
    - ***Avoidance:*** The unconscious fear that causes people to resist from something they assume will happen, even if they make their best effort.
    - ***People-pleasing:*** Giving, often at the expense of one's own needs or desires, with the hope of getting something unconsciously desired in return for the efforts.
    - ***Justification:*** The closed-minded effort to prove one's choices as right or reasonable.
    - ***Ruminating:*** An inability to give up self-righteousness or sad thoughts no matter what other information is presented.
    - ***Rationalization:*** Attempting to explain or justify behavior; or an attitude with logical reasons, even if these are not appropriate.
    - ***Gas-lighting***: Manipulating (someone) by psychological means into questioning their own sanity.

- **Reaction Formation**: An extreme denial in which someone behaves in the opposite way they actually feel.

Unfortunately, Level One 'Basement Dwellers' often go to doctors or therapists who get medication prescribed to them when they are anxious and depressed. In some cases, this may help them if they are chemically imbalanced. But often the people at this level of consciousness never do the work needed to uncover the deeper root cause: Their unconscious belief that they are not deserving; or lovable enough or capable enough. While medication may relieve some anxiety and depression, it will not help the patient to become more conscious of their decision-making.

As you can see, the ability to **manifest** is more difficult in level one consciousness, because there is a lot of reaction and unconsciousness of what one wants at this level. As a result of this unconsciousness, people at this level often feel like a victim. They believe the 'Universe' and 'God' are not supporting them, when the problem is that they are not conscious of what they want and the possibilities to get it. Those in this level of consciousness are often playing 'defense'; instead of "offense".

The **thoughts** of a Basement Dweller, constantly flip back and forth from "I am going to go for what I want!" to "I am not enough to get what I want!" These are the thoughts of the grandiose and self-doubt ego. With both thoughts, there is a claim, but no plan and substance behind the thoughts. As a result, it is based in unconscious illusion, not reality. The unconscious thoughts that swarm around in the mind of level one consciousness are as follows:

- I am not deserving of receiving what I say I want.
- I am not capable enough to get what I say I want.
- I am not lovable enough to be supported in what I want.
- God and the Universe will not support me in what I want.
- Life never works out for me.

Therefore, level one, Basement Dwellers, often are being controlled by the following unconscious **feelings**:
- Shame
- Guilt
- Grief
- Fear
- Apathy
- Anxiety
- Depression
- Separation
- Abandonment
- Powerlessness
- Insecurity
- Confusion
- Hopelessness

You know you are in level one consciousness, a Basement Dweller, if you have the following **behaviors:**

- Frequently gossip and talk about what others did or said or the faults in others; instead of looking at yourself.
- Prefer to have a Pollyanna-positive outlook on things, hoping the negatives in your life will magically go away and improve, instead of dealing with them.
- Worry and fret about what others may be doing or not doing; instead of realizing what you want to create and then stepping into your life to assert what you want.
- Procrastinate, instead of doing what you always say you want to do.
- Over-giving to others; instead of taking the time to figure out what you want and how you can give it to yourself.
- Being completely frozen, without any idea of how you feel or what you want.
- Spend time justifying your behavior versus seeking to understand how to get what you want.

- Constantly arguing and pushing because of your need to be right and in control.
- Limited thinking about your choices to get what you want.
- Act like a victim or persecutor.

The **results** for the Basement Dwellers are survival and existence for today. There is no plan or hope for the future. Life is about instant gratification.

The **benefit** for dwelling in this consciousness is as follows:
- It is mass consciousness; therefore, you feel connected to others in your unconscious wound-ology.
- You do not have to take personal responsibility or be accountable to anyone, including yourself.
- You don't have to do the work of awakening to your beliefs, thoughts, feelings and behaviors you choose as a result. Therefore, you can be a victim and persecute others.
- You live in the moment of instant gratification, instead of living with delayed gratification that would allow you to reach your vision, values, and goals.

While there are benefits to being a Basement-Dweller, remember this: The basement is dark, and it smells! Even if you remodel it and mask it with a dehumidifier, it is still a basement that is underground and therefore has a limited view! In the basement of your consciousness, you live without light shining in on what truly is your negative belief controlling your circumstances. In this level of consciousness, you blame the circumstances and others for how you feel; instead of looking deeper within yourself to your beliefs and thoughts. This protects your ego, that is full of pride and shame. Therefore, dwelling in the basement makes it difficult to self-reflect.

To begin to become more conscious of your beliefs and fears, begin to raise your level of consciousness, by spending time in nature. We will discuss this more in the next chapter.

Level Two: Self-Doubt and Judgment *(The Kitchen Experience)*

At this level of consciousness, you are now more aware of your feelings, which are full of Self-Doubt and Judgment. It feels painful to start to become conscious of the pride and shame that have been driving you up until now. In this stage of consciousness, you can either go backwards to numb the pride and shame; or you will go forward to greater self-awareness in the next level of consciousness.

The following **belief** is at work, causing the level 2 consciousness: "If only I had (blank), I could (blank)!"

At this level of consciousness, you are still looking outside of yourself for safety, security, love and belonging—wishing and wanting certain things externally that you believe are out of your reach. This could be what you wish others were doing; or what you wish you had.

At level two consciousness, your three brains are still out of synch. You have increased your Gut Intelligence™ (GQ) slightly, but your head is now front and center: chattering so much with self-doubt and judgment, that you are still having a hard time figuring out how to get what you want.

Here is what your gut, heart and head are doing at this level:

- **Gut**:
  You are becoming a bit less reactive when you get that gut-alert, but now that gut-alert is now triggering your chattering mind. Since your mind is now front and center, your fight and flight reaction has slowed down somewhat. Instead of trusting your gut, your gut acts as a switch to make your mind want to quickly judge: Who is right and who is wrong? This sometimes leads you to your self-doubt, while other times you think judgmental thoughts towards others.

- **Heart:**
  You are beginning to feel more conscious of what you don't want at this level. You still, however, have a lot of unconsciousness around what you feel and how to allow those feelings to guide you towards what you do want. As you try to open your heart and feel at this level, it feels a bit messy because you are in the unknown of what you want to create. This causes you to go in your chattering mind again, as you experience mostly self-doubt and judgment.

- **Head**
  Your head is front and center now, but not in a good way! It is chattering like crazy and full of self-doubt and judgment towards yourself and others. This is because you are still anxious and depressed because you believe you are not deserving; or lovable enough or capable enough to get what you want. At this level, you don't yet understand your self-doubt and judgment, you just know you have it.

Your greatest **defense mechanisms** at this level of consciousness are:

- Self-deprecation
- Judgment
- Switch and blame

At this level, while you feel a lot of self-doubt, you avoid deeper reflection of what that is all about and, therefore, do not like accountability. If someone points out what you are doing, you get very defensive because you have so much self-doubt. You may even use a defense mechanism like 'Switch and Blame' to judge the person who was holding you accountable to avoid a deeper reflection of yourself.

Because you are spending your energy on self-doubt and judgment, you have a difficult time **manifesting** what you want. This is because you know what you don't want and feel powerless to get what you want.

In this level of consciousness, your **thoughts** are pre-occupied with finding fault, instead of finding possibilities to the obstacles and problems that exist. What we focus on expands—so your focus is not giving you what you want. Much of this reason is because you are not spending time thinking about what you want. Instead, you are getting stuck in the drama of the blame-shame game.

The thoughts of someone in level two consciousness are:

- You think that what you need to get is outside of yourself.
- You think about who's at fault.
- You think others or circumstances are causing your current situation.
- You continually re-play the story in your head that "if only I had (blank), I could have what I want".
- In your mind you spin things the following way:
    - It's not my fault—I'm a victim of circumstances.
    - There's nothing I can do about it.
    - They made me feel this way.
    - It's not the right time to deal with it.
    - Someone needs to be judged: It's either me, them or God.
    - I can't seem to cut a break!
    - I am not enough.
    - They are not enough.

Furthermore, trying to place blame sets off your negative **feelings** that are swarming around in your heart. At this level, you do not know yet what you desire, as a feeling of powerlessness, anger, and fear overcome you. Level two: Kitchen Dwellers spend a lot of time talking about the drama in their lives at their kitchen table, instead of figuring out how they feel and what they want. Kitchen Dwellers mostly feel:

- Powerlessness (Self-doubt)
- Anger (Judgment)
- Fear (Self-doubt

At this level of consciousness, you likely are not addicted, however, your **behavior** is still full of distractions to dull your consciousness. These distractions may include:

- Co-dependent relationships
- People-pleasing
- Avoidance
- Busyness
- Perfectionism
- Drama: Caused by reactions of fight and flight

You know you are in level two consciousness, a 'Kitchen Dweller', if you have the following **behaviors**:

- Fight or flight reactions to what occurs.
- Frequently judge others, or yourself, quickly in a situation.
- Focus a lot on who is right and who is wrong.
- See things in very black and white terms.
- Waste a lot of time talking to others about your "dramas".
- Playing the "devil's advocate", focusing on fault, what went wrong, and what could go wrong.

Unfortunately, Kitchen-Dwellers don't often get the **results** they want easily! This is because they spend a lot of time cooking up stories about who is right and wrong! Most of the time their stories have a persecutor or victim storyline to them. Mostly you sense from their stories that they deeply believe: "If only I had this one ingredient, I could get what I want!"

It's not until the next level of consciousness, that there is an awakening to oneself and the possibilities that exist. At this level of consciousness, there is still a belief that circumstances, and people, are creating your thoughts, feelings, behavior, and results in your life. In summary, the Kitchen-Dwellers live in the drama of life, spending a lot of time as the critic.

Why do people stay at this level two consciousness? The **benefit** for dwelling in this consciousness is as follows:

- It is mass consciousness; therefore, you feel connected when you have conversations with others and play the victim/persecutor game.
- You don't have to do the work of awakening to your beliefs, thoughts, feelings and behaviors, so you can see why you have the results in your life.
- You get to be the judge and the critic! That makes you feel, at some level, in control and powerful, even though judging doesn't get you anywhere but on the thrown in your own mind!

But while there are benefits to be a Kitchen-Dweller, remember this: Sitting in the kitchen, stirring the pot, and eating that same 'ole meal repeatedly, makes you fat and unhealthy! Yes, you need to get out of the kitchen and see life from a different room. It's time to let go of being a victim or playing the role of the persecuting judger!

To help you get to the next level of consciousness: Pause and just breathe when you want to start thinking thoughts of self-doubt and judgment. You will learn more about this technique in the next chapter.

Level Three: Self-Awareness *(The Closet Experience)*

At this level of consciousness, you begin to observe and own your ego's grip on your consciousness. Yes, up until now your ego has been edging your greatest self out—your intuition! But now that you are becoming self-aware, you can just notice your ego's reaction before it gets the best of you!

You can observe your ego when you 'own' it with pure observation and curiosity. This means observing how you quickly go into a mindset of: Fear, judgment, and control. Your ego's-mindset makes you choose one of two behaviors: fight or flight. But, by observing your reaction with non-judgment and curiosity, you will begin to be able to stop yourself before you act out! Raising your level of consciousness in this way, puts you in the driver's seat and eventually allows you to choose how you want to respond, instead of reacting to situations.

Our **Belief** at this level is: "It is what it is! I am able to observe my desire to react with curiosity and non-judgment."

This belief reflects your self-awareness and acceptance of what your ego wants you to do without judgment. This is a stage of emotional neutrality. By observing your ego's desire to react, you can become curious about what the belief is behind the reaction. This will help reveal the unconscious belief that was once driving your reaction: Believing you were not deserving, not lovable enough or not capable enough and, therefore, susceptible to The Velcro Effect.

At level three consciousness, you become more conscious of what is going on in your three brains, thus increasing your Gut Intelligence™ (GQ). While each one is operating separately, and not in synch yet with one another, you are becoming aware of what is happening in each one:

- **Gut**:
  You are now consciously aware of that gut-alert! Yes, you are beginning to understand what the belief and fear is inside of you that is causing that instant reaction. To further your exploration, say to yourself, "Isn't that interesting...look how I want to react! I wonder what belief, thought and feeling is causing me to want to react?" By being curious and observing the desired reaction, you will become more self-aware of the unconscious belief that has been driving your reaction up until now. As you learn how to breathe more deeply into your gut, you will be able to disrupt the reaction and become more self-aware of what that gut-alert is all about.

- **Heart:**
  Now, focus on your heart. At this level, your heart is becoming more conscious. When you stop your gut-reaction and focus on observing what you fear, you will become more self-aware of the energy swirling around in your heart. Pause and breathe into it. Observe any Velcro-Effect, that might be going on. Consciously choose to unstick the stickiness that may be causing you to not feel deserving enough—lovable enough or capable enough. Now, stop focusing on your fear of not being enough and observe what you desire instead. What is it? Feel that as though you have it already.

- **Head:**
  Your mind is now playing the old fear on the big screen TV and the volume is turned up loud! There it is! Simply observe it now that you are self-aware that this is the movie that had been playing unconsciously in the background up until now. But remember, you are the movie theater director, so you get to change the movie, and turn down the volume anytime you wish. This will happen in the next level of consciousness, after you fully observe what is happening at this level. Pause and breathe deeply, as you simply keep observing what is.

At this level of consciousness, there are very few **defense mechanisms**, as you are focusing on self-awareness. Some people call this the level of mindfulness. In this level of consciousness, you have not replaced your beliefs, thoughts, feelings, and behaviors yet—but you have suspended your reaction to them! So, congratulations!

In this level of self-awareness, your observation and curiosity allow you to see you and understand how you have not felt enough, up until now. You are a 'Closet Dweller': Going into the dark closets in your house and observing what is all in there! It's been so long since you were in there, you didn't even know what was in the closet! Instead of being defensive when people tell you that your closets are messy, you simply want to observe what is in there and desire to get curious about how to make it better. This allows you to get out of denial and stand in your truth. You are not cleaning out the closet yet and making any changes—you are simply taking an inventory with more mindfulness so you can take personal responsibility. Getting to this level of consciousness helps you to understand how taking a personal inventory is much more productive than self-doubt and judgment.

While there is a great improvement in consciousness at this level, you are not **manifesting** yet! You are at the stage of awakening to how your ego has gotten in the way of your ability to manifest what you want. But you haven't figured out how to get the closet looking like you want it to yet! Now, in this closet-consciousness stage, it's not time to manifest yet; it's time to become self-aware of the old beliefs, thoughts, feelings and behaviors that have been holding you back. Currently, you are experiencing the following thoughts, feelings, and behaviors:

The **thoughts** of someone in level three consciousness are:

- I am able to be more self-aware, and non-judgmental, when I observe what is happening around me and within me.
- I am able to stop my reaction by simply observing the desire to react.
- I am able to get curious and wonder why I believe I am not enough.

Level three, Closet-Dwellers, have the following **feelings**:

- Desire
- Curiosity
- Courageousness
- Neutrality (Instead of judgment towards self and others)

While we are not quite sure what we desire to create yet; we do have the desire to stop reacting! This is a start! We also have the desire to be curious and learn more about our self. By courageously looking at yourself and your reactive tendencies, you become neutral and are no longer afraid to see what used to be in your blind-spot.

You know you are in level three consciousness, a Closet Dweller, if you have the following **behaviors**:

- You mostly pause before you react.
- You are breathing more deeply.
- You are observing yourself, with pure curiosity, and non-judgment.
- You contemplate your beliefs, thoughts, feelings, behavior, and results.
- You are equally as interested in being self-aware as you are the results in your life, so you are slower to speak and act.
- When you do speak and act, you are more intentional.
- You are less defensive when people hold you accountable or correct you.
- You are consciously spending more time in pure observation of self.
- You are becoming more self-aware of your reactions and simply observing them before they happen.
- You are beginning to wonder about how you would respond, instead of react.

By observing how you currently want to react, you slow down the reaction process, and begin to have a moment of choice. This moment of choice may leave you in the unknown, wondering what to do or say. That's progress—at least you are not reacting like you used to react!

This level of awareness helps you to step out of fear, so you can begin to detach from the negative beliefs that once drove you to a fight or flight reaction. These old reactions were due to your fear of what you imagined might happen if you exercised your authentic truth and voice.

Why do people stay at this level three consciousness? The **benefit** for dwelling in this consciousness is as follows:

- You increase your mindfulness and self-awareness.

- You discover the negative self-talk and beliefs that once drove your fight/flight behavior in a direction you did not want to go.
- You are starting to feel a sense of connection with yourself by accepting that part of you that reacted because it believed you were not deserving, capable, and lovable enough.
- You are now beginning to wonder what your authentic, and not reactive, voice would sound like if you told people how you felt and what you needed.
- You are starting to integrate your ego and your intuition by your pure, and non-judgmental, observations of yourself.

But while there are benefits in being a Closet-Dweller, remember this: The closet will eventually get messed up again. So, no matter how well you clean it out and organize it, you eventually must move on in your life and start living. When you do, the closet will likely get messy again! That's okay. You can always go back in it for further cleaning, organizing, and deciding what will stay and go!

Level Four: Detachment *(The Waiting Room Experience)*

At this level of consciousness, you have transformed your ego that wants to go into a fight or flight response. But now—you are sitting in 'The Waiting Room' before your intuition speaks to you! While this can be difficult, there are many ways you can shift in The Waiting Room. One of them is your belief system, which begins to be less focused on your deficits and more focused on being more open, trusting and allowing your intuition to guide you. In this stage you are detaching from your ego's grip, that used to run your life.

The **belief** at this level of consciousness is:

"This or something better is coming my way!"

This belief allows you to detach from your ego's grip on how things 'should' be and the outcomes you believed you must have in order to overcome your insecurities of being deserving, or not lovable, or capable enough. In this stage of detachment, you are becoming more open, trusting, and allowing of your intuition to lead your life. This means you are letting go of the ego's mindset of: Fear, judgment, and control.

Detaching from your ego's reaction and your stronghold on the outcomes of safety, security, love and belonging—you begin to just accept what is. This does not mean you are complacent. It means you are letting go of fear, judgment, and control. Now, you are replacing that mindset with becoming more open to what is—trusting the unfoldment—and allowing intuition to do the work in your life.

While you are not at the level of Intuitive Alignment yet, you are practicing being in the present moment with more trust as you sit in The Waiting Room with positive expectancy. Being in the present moment, also allows you to spend more time thinking about what it is you love and, therefore, want to create; versus what it is you fear.

At level four consciousness, you are operating at a higher level of increased your Gut Intelligence™ (GQ) because you are detaching from your old ego-scripts that limited you. Now, you are becoming more aware of how your gut, heart, and head are speaking to you. You are beginning to assign a role to each one, understanding that when they work together effectively, they act like a Board of Directors, guiding you to effective decision-making. Here are their roles

- **Gut**: Gut-alert signals that it's time to pay attention! You are now consciously aware of that gut-alert! And you understand that the gut-alert is simply a signal to tell you to pay attention. That's all! You no longer react when you get a gut-alert. You simply pause and breathe, so you can pay attention. In this stage of consciousness, you also immediately envision that you are strong and intuitive to handle whatever comes your way! Your gut knows—you've got this! Your gut is your sense of personal power.

- **Heart:** Your heart aligns you to what you want!
  At this level of consciousness, you know that your heart aligns you to what you want. So, after you get that gut-alert that tells you, "It's time to pay attention!", you ask your heart what it desires. By listening to the emotions of your heart, when you envision different scenarios, you will know which scenario is right for you. Your heart, at this level of consciousness, aligns you to what you want.

- **Head:** At this level of consciousness, your head assimilates how you will get what you want!
  In this level 4: Detachment, your mind works for you to assimilate the unconscious and conscious facts so that you can imagine the possibilities to get what you want. You do this by detaching from your fear and being more open, trusting and allowing the possibilities to come to you. At this stage, you work on envisioning what you want.

While you are aware of the different roles of the gut, heart, and head, at this level of consciousness, The Waiting Room, you are practicing these roles so in the next level they can be more synchronistic.

There are usually no **defense mechanisms** at this level of consciousness because you are detached from your ego's scripts and reactions. You are now in a problem-solving mode, wondering how you will realize what you are envisioning.

Sometimes, however, an old negative belief or fear will arise. When it does, just consciously choose to go back down the elevator and visit floor 3: Self-Awareness. This is where you must go clean out the closet again a bit more. Once you have completed level 3: Self-Awareness, focus on what you want to create, not what you fear, and this will get you to Level 4: Detachment once again. It's as simple as that! When I find myself down at the lower levels of consciousness again, I allow myself 24-hours to get back up, so I'm intentional and don't wallow in lower levels of consciousness.

As you can see, Level 4: Detachment is a transformational level of consciousness. That is why it can feel like you are having a 'Waiting Room' Experience. In the Waiting Room, you are not yet **manifesting** because you are working on something different: Detaching from your ego, so your intuition can take front and center.

In this stage, you are like a butterfly, waiting to be set free, but still in the cocoon, wrestling to get out. You are pushing up against the walls of your mind as you struggle with 'My will' verses 'Thine will'. 'My will' is all of your ego's attachments to safety, security, love and belonging. When you wrestle with your ego-scripts, that make you believe you 'NEED' certain things to be enough, you will raise you level of consciousness about what you believed made you safe, secure, loved and belonging to a group. In this stage, you realize that there is a big difference between 'need and want'. In this stage of Detachment, you wrestle with this paradigm shift and orientation in your life. It is in this level of consciousness you choose to surrender 'My Will' to 'Thine will'. 'Thine will' refers to surrendering to something bigger than yourself. This could mean your ego-self, higher consciousness, your intuition, the Holy Spirit within you, or God—whatever you chose to call it.

The **thoughts** of someone in this level of consciousness is more open, trusting, and allowing these ego-scripts to be challenged. By challenging what we learned from our parents and society, we can then choose to let that go, so we can surrender to the Intuitive Inner Voice, which is our authentic truth.

Those in The Waiting Room, in level four consciousness, have the following **feelings**:

- Willingness
- Letting Go
- Acceptance
- Reason

While it may seem like it takes a lot of time in The Waiting Room to get what you want, the purpose of The Waiting Room is to solidify the shift in mindset from:

- Fear, judgment, and control (Ego)
- Open, trusting and allowing (Intuition)

At Level 4: Detachment, you become clearer about what you want, as you let go of these ego-scripts of what you think you 'should' want for your life. You know you have arrived at Level 4 consciousness when you do the following **behaviors**:

- Forgive yourself for believing the illusions of safety, security, love, and belonging were outside of yourself in the ways you learned.
- Forgive others for teaching you that safety, security, love, and belonging were outside of yourself in the way they believed.
- Let go and detach from societal and group norms, without judgment, to self or others.
- Let go of any deeper fears and attachments you are still holding onto that make you want to believe that safety, security, love, and belonging are outside of you.
- Enjoy "The Waiting Room" as a time to really get to know yourself and what you truly value and want—this is the magic of "The Waiting Room". (Trust me: In the next level you will then be manifesting if you use this time wisely!).

The **result** of level four consciousness is detaching from your ego and beginning to align to your intuition.

Why do people stay at this level four consciousness? The **benefit** for dwelling in this consciousness is as follows:

- You become free of the illusions that safety, security, love and belonging exist outside of yourself.

- You forgive yourself, and others, for the illusions that the power you needed to create safety, security, love, and belonging was actually outside of yourself.
- You begin to really get to know and love yourself, including accepting what you truly love and want.
- You detach from your ego and begin to align to your intuition, so that 'Thine will' is 'My will'.
- You begin to focus more inwardly on getting your gut, heart, and head in synch so you can better listen to what each one is guiding you to do.
- You spend this time in The Waiting Room to develop your vision, values, and goals.

Level Five: Intuitive Alignment *(The Rooftop Experience)*

At this level of consciousness, you are now detached from your ego and aligned to your Intuitive Inner Voice! Congratulations! Just remember though: This is not a destination. This is a journey. That means while you are no longer run by the illusions that once ran your life, you could slip back from time to time. While you now know these illusions are entrapments that keep you from being truly connected to your authentic self, you will sometimes miss them and want to re-visit them again. When you do, it will be good, as you will realize they are illusions and, therefore, not fulfilling as you once remembered they were.

In level 5, you realize that your Intuitive Inner Voice is your authentic voice. It is your higher consciousness, not some 'authority' outside yourself that is trying to run your life. That is why you begin to understand: 'Thine will' is actually 'My will'. As a result, there is no struggle to surrender any longer, because you know that when you surrender, you receive the synchronicity only your intuition can offer.

Now your **belief** is 'I AM one with the Divine. I AM a vessel of truth and love. I have all that I need; therefore, that which I observe shifts.'

Because you are now focused on what you envision for your life, your values, and goals—you can have a "Rooftop Experience" that allows you to see things from a higher perspective. This means you don't fall into the mass consciousness of fear, judgment and control any longer. Nor do you strive and drive to get where you want to go. Instead, you surrender.

Surrender means you are at the highest level of Gut Intelligence™ (GQ). At this level, you know what is going on in your gut, heart, and head and these three brains are in synch, like an effective Board of Directors.

At this level of consciousness, the following is occurring:

- **Gut:**
  You get a simple gut-alert that tells you to pay attention. You then say to yourself, "Isn't that interesting, I wonder what that is all about?" As you pause and breathe, you observe what is happening around you and within you with pure curiosity.

- **Heart:**
  Next, you ask your heart what it feels. If it feels anxious, you trust something is not right for you. If you feel angry, you know there is something you need to change. If you are disappointed, you know you need to assert yourself and your expectations. If you are hurt, you know you need to share what you want and set boundaries on what is not acceptable for you. If you are happy, you express your gratitude. If you feel love, you let others know. And if you desire something, you simply ask for it and go for it.

- **Head:**
  At this level of consciousness, you use your mind to envision what you want. You don't have to spend time wondering what you want—you already did all of that in Level Four. Because you know what you want, you can practice The Heisenberg Theory: That which we focus on shifts. So, realizing this physics theory,

you focus on what you want—not what you fear. (You will learn more about The Heisenberg Theory in the upcoming chapters).

- **Intuition:**
  And finally, after seeing it in your mind's eye, you surrender it to your intuition. This means you engage in a partnership with your intuition by asking, "How might I get what I want?" Instead of doing this occasionally, you do it continually throughout the day, as though your intuition was a partner working right alongside of you. When you hear guidance, you immediately step in and trust. This means you don't just ask your intuition for wisdom, and don't follow through. You have the guts to do something about it, so you do follow through with what you now know is your truth.

When you awaken to this level of consciousness, you believe that any resistance you experience is only a reflection of the resistance within—your fear. Resistance within is caused by your attachments to the outcome, the fear that you may not get what you want, and the belief that you are not enough. You no longer have this resistance because you have cleared out all those fears, attachments to the outcomes and negative beliefs about yourself.

This allows you to focus on The Heisenberg Theory: That which you observe shifts. This is a physics theory that explains how powerful you are at manifesting when you are free of fear and know in your gut, heart, and mind—your truth. As you observe that truth, without any incongruency within yourself, you will execute whole-heartedly without fear and, therefore, will create what you desire.

This is because you do not have any **defense mechanisms**, based on fear, that are holding you back from creating what you want.

As a result, at this level of consciousness, you are able to **manifest**!!! Whooooo-hoooo! Yes, when you are in Intuitive Alignment, you are clear of your fear and ready to manifest that which you envision. You are now in the flow and life becomes synchronistic for you!

Say for example, you want a connected relationship with someone in your family or someone at work. Let's say that they are not allowing you into what is happening in their life and you can sense their disconnection by how they abruptly answer questions and avoid deeper conversation with you. Instead of going into the lower level conscious of fear, judgment, and control—which will create resistance—you can choose to be at level 5 consciousness and just be more open, trusting, and allowing the connection to unfold.

When you are at Level 5, you observe things as they are, and practice pure curiosity. This helps you to be in a state of wonder: Observing what is and observing what you want to create. The more you are open, trusting, and allowing your intuition to guide you—you will just know what is happening and what you need to do about it. Instead of getting caught up in fear, judgment and the attempt to control your situation—you just continue to stay curious about what you need to do or say, while you hold your vision in your mind and send this person love, not fear. This allows you to create openness, not resistance. This is the power of The Heisenberg Theory: That which we observe shifts.

By knowing in your gut, heart and mind this truth: I AM able to shift that which I observe—you will observe what is happening from your highest self which is love—not from your ego, which is fear. This means you won't try to control it; nor will you take anything personally. This is because you don't believe you have to have a certain outcome, in a certain timing, to be okay. By simply feeling love and observing what you want to shift—you begin to co-create a different experience.

Your ego's fear and judgment are no longer getting in the way and causing resistance and drama from your unconscious storylines you used to project onto situations. At this level of consciousness, you realize that all you want, you already have because you know—that which I observe shifts. This is reality because illusions are created when you believe the power is outside of yourself. Therefore, this is how you think, feel, and behave at this level of consciousness:

Your main **thoughts** are:

- Hmmm…isn't that interesting, I wonder….
- How might I get (blank)?
- I AM a vessel of what I say I want (is it love, abundance, openness?)
- That which I observe shifts

At this level of consciousness, no longer are you operating from your **feelings** of fear and deprivation that you may not get what you want. Instead, you are "acting as if" you have everything you want, because everything you want is unfolding in perfect timing. This means you feel:

Love
Joy
Peace
Passion
Enlightenment
Power

At this level, you realize that the amount of Love, Joy, Peace, Passion, Enlightenment and Power you experience has nothing to do with what you have or what is currently unfolding in your life. It is a matter of consciousness.

In fact, the more you believe you are a vessel of the Intuitive Inner Voice flowing through you, which some call "The I AM Presence"—the better your chances are of actually creating the life you want. This is because you no longer long for anything! You believe you deserve it and already have all the safety, security, love and belonging you need! The rest is just the cherry on your sundae! And if anything, or anyone, melts your whip cream—you observe it and shift that fast!

And, that which you observe shifts—because you will step in as an advocate for yourself to make whatever changes you need to be make—to love yourself well! And know, as we love our self well, we set others free to do the same.

Now, that you are in the highest level of consciousness, you no longer struggle with what **behavior** you "should" do. Where once it was a battle between your ego and your Intuitive Inner Voice, you now are completely aligned to your intuition, As a result, you:

- Surrender to a higher level of consciousness, your Intuitive Inner Voice that transcends your chattering ego (which is fear-based).
- Trust what you are being guided on what to do or say.
- Focus on gratitude, realizing that which you long for you already have in abundance and is unfolding in perfect timing, for your higher good.
- Focus on love and speaking the truth in love.
- Make decisions that are in alignment with your vision, values, and goals—no matter how others might react.
- Count your blessings in the present moment, instead of wishing and wanting things to be different.

At this level of consciousness, you are getting the **results** you want! This is because your ego, which used to be full of fear, is no longer controlling you! Because your greatest goal and intention is to be aligned with your Higher Consciousness, you don't interfere when you are not getting what you think you want, when you think you want it. You are open, trusting, and continue to allow your intuition to guide you, and supply you, in each and every moment. This means you stay in the present moment and count the blessings you have now, instead of always yearning for more.

The **benefit** of living at this level of consciousness, the Rooftop Experience, is you are free from fear and illusions! This means you are not afraid to hear the truth; or speak your truth in love. This allows you to have a more authentic relationship with others that is not predicated on manipulation of the outcome.

As you have just learned in this chapter, when you elevate your consciousness, you let go of the old ego-scripts that tell you how you 'should' be, think, and act. This allows you to become more open, trusting, and allowing of your intuition to guide you. As you learn to quiet your ego's chattering mind, and awaken to your intuitive still small voice instead, you begin to have a deeper connection with your authentic self. That is the benefit of elevating your consciousness—you now begin to make decisions that are exactly right for you! Now, that is flying free my friend!

Even after you arrive at Level 5: Intuitive Alignment, know that there will be times that things happen or are said that will throw you down into the lower levels of consciousness once again. Sometimes you will not feel like you chose to be in that lower level of consciousness. Instead, it will feel like someone threw you in the elevator and pressed floor one or two for you! When that happens—be grateful! Yes, be grateful that you are now doing the deeper work that kept you stuck in some unconscious belief and fear that was likely getting in the way of you manifesting what you want, without you even knowing! And now that you are thrown into this lower level of consciousness, you can do the work to clear any negative or limited belief that is still holding you back from your potential. We will talk more about how to do that in the next chapter.

But first, remember The Velcro Effect we talked about in the previous chapter? When you get thrown into a lower level consciousness, it is because someone found a sticky-point in you. This sticky point is a fear or self-doubt you are still carrying around about yourself that has now been exposed. While it may have felt like they did this on purpose, don't focus on their motive. Focus on the level of consciousness you currently are in, so you can elevate your consciousness and get to the 5th floor of Intuitive Alignment once again!

You know you are at a lower level of consciousness again if you react in one of the following ways:

- Get defensive
- Need to prove yourself to someone
- Start striving and driving
- Justify yourself
- Over-convince someone you are right
- Change yourself to accommodate their expectations
- Switch and Blame
- Quietly judge them
- Flee from the situation altogether
- Fight to prove your point

To illustrate this point, imagine that someone called you, 'A two-headed green monster'. Would you believe them? Of course not! But if they told you that you were scary to them, like a two-headed monster, because you were so intuitive and strong, you might get triggered into The Velcro Effect. This would only happen if you had self-doubt and judgment about your intuition and strength. But if you did not have any self-doubt or judgment towards yourself in this way, you would likely be simply curious as to why they said what they did. Notice, when we are not experiencing The Velcro Effect, it is because we are practicing curiosity, instead of self-doubt and judgment.

Now that you have learned about the 5 Levels of Consciousness, in the next chapters you will learn about the 5 Practices to Elevate your Consciousness. By doing these steps on a regular basis, you will ground yourself in your intuitive knowing, so you are prepared to notice the cues at the tip of the iceberg, when needed. This will allow you to become an Intuitive Leader, in all aspects of your life!

Chapter Four:
5 Practices to Elevate your Consciousness

Now that you have learned how to elevate your consciousness and experience, let's look at the 5 Practices to Elevate your Consciousness, so that you can ground yourself and align to your intuition. By grounding yourself and aligning to your intuition, you will be prepared to notice the cues at the tip of the iceberg and pivot quickly, if necessary. This means you will be clear, calm, and confident in taking risks and negotiating your viewpoints with others because you will be able to effectively articulate your gut's knowing, your heart's desires; and the possibilities that exist to meet your vision, values and goals! This will prepare you to become an effective Intuitive Leader, which we will talk about in more detail in the upcoming chapters.

The 5 Practices to Elevate your Consciousness, are:

Practice #1: Be in Nature

Practice #2: Pause and Breathe

Practice #3: Observe and Meditate

Practice #4: Envision

Practice #5: Surrender

People ask me if they can do all these steps no matter what level of consciousness they are in, and the answer is "yes, but...". The "yes" is that you can do these steps to raise your level of consciousness. The "but" refers to the fact that the practices are harder to do if you are not in that corresponding level of consciousness.

So, let's begin with each practice, understanding that likely you will be corresponding these practices in the following levels of consciousness:

Level One: Unconsciousness:
Start to *spend more time in nature* to get connected with yourself. This could be sitting in your backyard, going for a walk, hiking, biking, kayaking, boating, gardening, or any activity that helps you to be connected to nature.

Level Two: Self-Doubt and Judgment:
When you *pause and breathe,* you interrupt your thoughts of self-doubt and judgment. As you practice pausing and breathing more deeply into your gut when you feel self-doubt and judgment, you will quiet your chattering mind that tells you that you are not enough, or neither is someone or something else.

Level Three: Self-Awareness:
Start to **observe** your desire to react. Notice exactly what you are believing, thinking, feeling and how you want to behave. **Spend 20-minutes a day in meditation** to improve your gut-brain axis. This will change the neuropathway from the emotional center to the executive functioning part of your brain..

Level Four: Detachment:
As you detach from your ego's reaction and the outcomes you that you needed to succeed, you will now have space and time to **envision** what it is you truly want to create in your life. Use this time to create a vision board, as well as your vision, values, and goals.

Level 5: Intuitive Alignment:
Now that you have let go of your ego's grip on the steering wheel of your life, and you've taken the time to figure out what you want—it's time to **surrender** to your Intuitive Inner Voice to guide you. Use the practices in the lower levels of consciousness on a regular basis, along with the question, "How might I...?" to quiet your mind and listen to your intuition's guidance.

As you can see, it would be difficult to do the 5th practice without doing the ones before them. Each practice and level of consciousness prepares you for the next level. But, once you get to the higher levels and practices, be sure to continue to do the practices in the lower levels to stay grounded.

Next, you will find more details on how to do these practices, so you can elevate your consciousness. Use this chapter as a workbook so you can hold yourself accountable to growth.

Workbook:
5 Practices to Elevate your Consciousness

STEP #1:
BE IN NATURE

Want one simple way to improve your level of consciousness? Then, spend time in nature daily. This could be sitting or being active—it doesn't matter: Being in nature has a way of helping us to be more in the present moment. We all prefer different aspects of nature, which is all around us when we are outside. Choose the form of nature that most suits you whether that is the mountains, woods, or water.

When spending time in nature, it's okay to be still or active. But if you choose to be active, get out of your head and stop worrying about if you are getting enough steps in or performing at a certain pace! Just be in the moment and take in the fresh air and nature. This includes having a sensory experience, such as the following:

- Sight: Tune into nature. See the tapestry of colors and how nature is harmonious.
- Sound: Notice the sounds of the birds, wind, and nature.
- Smell: Take in the smells of the air and your surroundings.
- Feeling: Feel the temperature, air, sun, and breeze on your body!
- Sensing: Just open up to the present moment and take in all that is!

Being in nature helps us to get out of our busy mind and instead be in the present moment. When we are in our busy mind, we are often unconscious about what is going on around us and in us. Our mind chatters, telling us we are not enough to get it all done! Suddenly, everything seems urgent, as though the house is on fire, when it is just a simple email that needs a response—whenever we can get to it! Just 20-minutes a day, in nature, can quiet your chattering mind and help you raise your level of consciousness.

Once you're done being in nature, then journal. This will help you to capture any awareness that came to you when you stepped away from your computer and to do list. While you may struggle at first with stepping away from being a 'human-doing', you will quickly learn that this time in nature will bring important realizations to you. Be free-flowing and write about anything that comes into your awareness!

JOURNAL

What area of your life did you think about when you were in nature?

- Relationships_____

- Vocation_____

- Financial_____

- Physical_____

- Mental_____

- Emotional_____

- Spiritual_____

What thoughts came into your mind?

What might you do about those thoughts?

STEP #2:
PAUSE & BREATHE

Stuff happens. People say and do things—and sometimes we can take what they say and do and run with it in our mind. We can often create a big story and drama from just a simple statement or action! But when you learn to pause and just breathe in the middle of the stuff, you will automatically raise your level of consciousness. This will help you to stop your chattering mind that makes you think thoughts of self-doubt and judgment.

Science tells us that pausing to breathe more deeply helps us to improve our gut-brain axis in many ways. First, it lowers our brainwave from beta to alpha. This gets our heart and brain in synch. Secondly, pausing for the practice of deeper breathing, also activates the bridge in the brain called the corpus callosum and makes it more efficient. This allows us to bring the neurons, neurotransmitters, and hormones from our gut, up the vagus nerve to our heart and head! This improves our Gut Intelligence™ (GQ).

Yes, by creating a better gut-brain axis you start to become aware of what is happening in your gut, heart, and head. While initially you may hear and sense a lot of self-doubt and judgment, this is all part of the growth process of identifying negative beliefs that are getting in the way of you manifesting the life you want to create, at work and home.

When pausing to breathe more deeply, do not worry about anything! Just focus on your breath and tune into your gut, heart, and head to become more conscious of what is going on inside of you. You likely have a lot of chattering going on, telling you how you are not deserving, capable, or lovable enough. At other times, you are projecting these same fears onto others and judging them. Just pause and breathe, noticing all of that.

As you begin to learn how to pause and breathe more deeply, this will eventually bring you to the next level of consciousness: Self-Awareness.

PRACTICE PAUSING & DEEP-BREATHING

Find a comfortable chair to sit in. Place your feet on the floor. Now, gradually breathe down to your belly in the following way:

- Breathe 3 times in your nose and out your mouth at the top of your chest.
- Repeat at the middle of your chest.
- Now bring your breath down to the top of your gut.
- Now bring your breath to the middle of your gut.
- Now bring your breath to the base of your body.

Make sure to breathe through your nose and out through your mouth 3 times at each area. It's best to take each breath as slowly as you can go. Now, once you've completed your breathing, (and of course you are still out in nature everyday), then start journaling to become more conscious of your self-doubt and judgment!

JOURNAL

1) Be honest: what thoughts of self-doubt and judgment are swarming in your head?

2) What beliefs do you think these thoughts are reflecting (Are you not deserving, lovable or capable enough?)

3) Where did this negative belief come from? (Think back to birth to eight years old)

STEP #3:
OBSERVE AND MEDITATE

Now that you have practiced being in nature, as well as pausing and breathing more deeply, it's time to take it to the next level: Observe what is happening around you and in you by pausing throughout the day to get curious and observe what is happening.

When you get curious to observe what is happening, you notice that gut-alert that is telling you to pay attention! Observing, without judgment, sounds something like this, "Isn't that interesting, my gut-alert is telling me that something is off. What is it?"

When we pause to observe that gut-alert, we take in the information more consciously, instead of rushing past it. Learn to observe what is happening around you when you get that gut-alert, so you don't miss important cues at the tip of the iceberg. Then, meditate 20-mintues a day to engage your intuition heightening your awareness and solving any concerns and problems you may have, because of your observation.

When you meditate 20-minutes a day you will change your brain! Science tells us that meditating 20-mintues a day will create a neuropathway that's like a four-lane highway to the executive center of our brain. This means you will no longer operate out of the emotional center of your brain, the amygdala, that puts you into fight or flight reaction. Creating this new neuropathway takes 20-minutes a day and about 3 weeks. You can split the 20-minutes up into two mediation sessions, or you can do one long one.

By meditating 20-minutes a day, you are beginning to acknowledge that there is an Intuitive Inner Voice that you want to consult, before making decisions. Intuition will only speak to you if you invite it in. So, be sure to invite your intuition in daily, during your meditation, for optimal results!

Keep in mind, that meditation is different than prayer. Often when people pray, they talk to God and tell God their concerns, as well as asking for help. In meditation, we ask our intuition an extremely focused problem-solving question, and then listen deeply by quieting our mind through deep breathing. This allows us to connect with our intuition in one of three ways:

- Visually: intuition often comes to us visually; through images and words we see.
- Auditorily: intuition can also come to us in a still small voice.
- Kinesthetic: intuition can also come to us through our body—a chill or a gut-alert.

Now, that you have been pausing to breath more deeply, observing your gut-alert and what is happening around you and within you, begin to meditate 20-minutes a day.

20-MINUTE MEDITATION PRACTICE

Find a comfortable chair to sit with your feet on the ground and back supported. Now, breathe in your nose and out your mouth 3 times, as slowly as you can, at each of these areas in your body:

- Upper chest
- Heart area
- Top of diaphragm
- Middle of diaphragm
- Lower diaphragm

(The above exercise is like the deep breathing exercise you did in the last session. You will now be adding onto it with a meditation).

Once you breathe in and out of these areas, as slowly as you can, then ask yourself a question to engage your intuition. This will help you to practice listening to your intuition.
Be sure to start your question with this phrase:

"How might I (what is it you want to know)?"

Make to ask only one question at a time, in one simple sentence like above. Once you have formed your question, continue to breathe deeply into your gut and do the following meditation:

- Visually: Look up into the right side of your mind's eye and ask: What do I see?
- Auditorily: Then, after you have stayed there awhile, bend to your left ear and ask: What do I hear?
- Kinesthetically: After you listened to that internal still small voice, look down to your gut and ask: What do I know for sure?

Go back around one more time, but this time in the opposite direction and listen, look, and sense in your gut what you know.

Now, after you are done with your meditation, journal below about what you saw, heard and sensed in your gut:

STEP 4:
ENVISION

Now that you have become more self-aware through observation and meditation, it is time to detach from your ego's grip. In this level of consciousness, Level 4: Detachment, we do the work of realizing and creating our vision, values, and goals—personally and professionally.

As we become clearer about what we want to create, in the seven areas of our life, we develop a compass for decision-making. The 7 Areas of our Life are:

- Vocationally
- Financially
- Relationally
- Emotionally
- Mentally
- Physically
- Spiritually

Creating a vision, values, and goals for the 7 Areas of Your Life, will help you to have a target for your decisions so you can create the life you want to live, at work and home. Use the prior meditation exercise to engage your intuition in creating these goals. Then, as you are living out your life, continue to engage your intuition to guide you in effective decision-making. This is how we develop a true partnership with our intuition.

To begin developing this partnership, do these two exercises:

1) A Vision Board;
2) Worksheet on your Vision, Values and Goals.

Keep in mind: This is best done when you have spent time in nature, have paused and breathed deeply to consider what you want, and have even meditating 20-minutes a day on these areas of your life. By doing these two exercises, in partnership with your intuition, you will be more apt to create a Vision Board and your Vision, Values and Goals from an authentic perspective, instead of your ego, that tells you what you "should" be doing.

Before you chart out your vision, values, and goals in the upcoming worksheet—do a Vision Board for both your personal and professional life. This will help you to engage your intuition in the process first, so you see what your unconscious mind is telling you that you want.

VISION BOARD EXERCISE

1) Buy poster board.
2) Get some of your favorite magazines.
3) Ask your Intuition, "What do I want to create next year?" (Focus on all 7 areas of your life: Vocationally, Financially, Relationally, Emotionally, Mentally, Physically, Spiritually).
4) Take a deep breath and let go of thinking about it as you page through the magazines.
5) Use the power of your subconscious mind as you rip out the words and pictures that make you feel good and jump off the page at you.
6) Now that you have enough to fill up your poster board, take what you ripped out and glue stick the images/words on a poster board. Do not worry where to place it, just let your instinct decide.
7) Look at your board filled and ask yourself: What does it tell me that I really want to create?
8) Ask yourself: What do I believe might be getting in the way of me creating that which I want?
9) Now that you are more self-aware of your desires, put your desires in the vision, values and goal format below.

VISION, VALUES AND GOALS WORKSHEET

Vision: (This is the "WHY" you do what you do)

What vision do you want for your personal/professional life? (do one for each)

This should be one sentence to capture your why you do what you do. For example, my vision is: *"To help people increase their Gut Intelligence (GQ) so they can manifest their vision, values and goals and, therefore, live a fulfilling life."*

Now, your turn. What is your vision?

"To…."

Values: (This reflects your character and "WHO" you are. Name 5-8 things that are important for you to be).

GOALS: (This reflects "what" you will do to reach your vision).

PERSONAL: Name a high-level goal for each of the following areas of your life and then 3 action steps, and timelines for each:

Relational: _____
What will you do: *When will you do it by:*

1)
2)
3)

Vocational: _____
What will you do: *When will you do it by:*

1)
2)
3)

Financial: _____
What will you do: *When will you do it by:*

1)
2)
3)

Physical: _____
What will you do: *When will you do it by:*

1)
2)
3)

Emotional: _____
What will you do: *When will you do it by:*

1)
2)
3)

Mental: _____
What will you do: *When will you do it by:*

1)
2)
3)

Spiritual: _____
What will you do: *When will you do it by:*

1)
2)
3)

If you are a manager or entrepreneur, you will want to do the Professional Goal Exercise on the next few pages. But even if you are an employee, and not in management, you will want to give this exercise a try! When I go into companies, I often work with the employees to align their job descriptions to the company goals. It's an intuitive exercise to ask yourself,

"How might I align what I do in my job, to contribute to the company goals?" When you really think about it, every job, and every department, needs to align to the company goals. Charting out your goals at work, in this way, will help you to use your intuition at work to make effective decisions.

Most managers unfortunately, however, do not do this exercise with their talent. When they don't—they get the polarization previously discussed. In companies this polarization is called: The Silo Effect. So, if your manager has not done this exercise with you—get empowered, and just do it for yourself. And then show it to them so they can see how you will spend your time and determine your priorities. Being proactive, like this, makes you an Intuitive Leader!

PROFESSIONAL: If you are in management, or you are an entrepreneur, you will surely want to name a high-level goal for each of the following areas of your work and then 3 action steps, and timelines for each: But even if you are an employee, pull out your job description and ask your intuition: "How might I align what I do in my job, to contribute to the company goals?"

Culture: _____
What will you do: *When will you do it by:*
1)
2)
3)

Sales: _____
What will you do: *When will you do it by:*
1)
2)
3)

Customer Service: _____
What will you do: *When will you do it by:*

1)
2)
3)

Teamwork/Operations: _____
What will you do: *When will you do it by:*

1)
2)
3)

Innovation: _____
What will you do: *When will you do it by::*

1)
2)
3)

Technology: _____
What will you do: *When will you do it by:*

1)
2)
3)

Marketing/Brand Alignment: _____

What will you do: *When will you do it by:*

1)
2)
3)

Now, when you are done with your goals, move on to the next Step #5: Surrender, on the following page.

STEP #5:
SURRENDER

Throughout the day, as stuff occurs, you can connect with your intuition when you surrender in the present moment. Surrendering means the following:

- You cease to resist and submit to our intuition for guidance.
- You give up the obstacles you were putting in the way because you thought you were not deserving or enough.
- You let go of your judgments: What you perceived was good, bad, right, wrong, needed, helpful or limiting.
- You asked for help, by asking, "How might I...?".
- You believe there is something bigger at work that can help you synchronize what you need so you can step into the flow.
- You receive what comes to you as a blessing, even if it is different than the form you expected.

You can surrender at any time throughout the day as stuff is happening. This means you do not have to wait until you get home to do your meditation to surrender. Instead, you can use the 60-second S.T.O.P. Technique to connect with your intuition in the moment you want to surrender your decision-making to your intuition.

Use the following 60-second S.T.O.P. Technique anytime you get a gut-alert that tells you to pay attention. Then, do this technique to invite your intuition in to help you:

60-SECOND S.T.O.P. TECHNIQUE EXERCISE

60-Second S.T.O.P. Technique

S-Slow down and breathe

T-Tune in to that gut-alert!

O-Observe what is happening

P-Perceive a new possibility to create the life you love by asking your intuition, "How might I (name what you want to manifest?"

Remember:
That which you observe shifts!!!

By using the 60-second S.T.O.P. Technique, you become open, trusting, and allowing of your intuition to guide you when you need it most. Of course, practice makes perfect! The first several times you use this technique, it may seem as though you detached from the stress, but are in The Waiting Room, without an answer yet. This is because you are strengthening your gut-brain axis. Just like weightlifting: The more you do it the stronger you get. Suddenly, after practicing the 60-second

S.T.O.P. Technique throughout the day, you will be able to get the answers you need immediately.

Once you are done doing the 60-second S.T.O.P. Technique, use the Journal below to get clear on what you need to do or say. If you are in a situation where others are around, you can still do the S.T.O.P. Technique, without them knowing. You don't have to close your eyes to do the S.T.O.P. Technique. When you are done, ask yourself these questions so you get clear on what to do or say. The more you journal, the more you will have these questions memorized and will be able to ask yourself them intuitively.

JOURNAL:

What was your gut-alert about?

What did your Intuition tell you to do or say when you did the 60-second S.T.O.P. Technique?

What will you choose to do or say as a result of this intuitive awareness?

In addition to the 60-second S.T.O.P. Technique and Journal, use these AFFIRMATIONS throughout the day to stay out of fear, and remind yourself of your connection to your intuition:

I AM Grateful
I AM Mindful
I AM Safe
I AM Secure

I AM Loved
I AM Connected
I AM Deserving
I AM Enough
I AM Truth
I AM Love
I AM Awake
I AM Beautifully and Wonderfully made
I AM Divine

In summary: When you think you are too busy to do the 5 Practices to Elevate your Consciousness, remember that spending the time doing these activities will help you become more clear, calm, and confident. Think of all the time you spend second-guessing yourself, calling someone to vent, or plopping yourself in front of your TV—just so you can become unconscious with that glass of wine or beer you are practically guzzling down!

Imagine instead, if you did the following 5 Practices to Elevate your Consciousness, how you would benefit. You would save time and agony if you would:

- Be in nature
- Pause and Breathe
- Observe and Meditate
- Envision
- Surrender

With the above practices, you will realize and develop the belief that intuition is there to:
- Assist you in becoming your authentic self.

- Guide you in everyday decision-making.
- Create synchronicity for you, so that things are more effortless and flow.
- Help you be more clear, calm, and confident no matter what is happening around you.
- Help you to have the wisdom to know the truth and guts to do something about it.
- Help you to be unattached to the outcome so you can accept whatever is thrown your way.

As you do the 5 Practices to Elevate your Consciousness on a regular basis, you will break free from your fear so you can awaken to your intuition.

In the next chapter, you will learn why Gut Intelligence™ (GQ) is the missing piece in leadership and how it is as important as IQ and EQ.

Chapter Five:
GQ is the Missing Piece

We have IQ and EQ, but when we are in the higher levels of consciousness, we have GQ. GQ is Gut Intelligence™: The missing piece to a fulfilling life; and the missing piece to effective leadership. GQ is the wisdom to know the truth at the tip of the iceberg before it's too late to pivot. It is the guts to do something about it when others are still gathering their data because they are afraid to take a risk. It can be applied in your personal life, as well as your professional life, to help you make effective decisions that align to the life you want to live.

By listening to your gut, heart, head—and surrendering to your intuition—you get all the information you need to succeed. But the best part is this success is your definition, not someone else's definition of success. Remember: You have your plan all laid out already! You did this while you were in Level 4 consciousness: The Waiting Room. And I'm sure you used the worksheet in the previous chapter to help guide you as well. In addition, I know you meditated on it, using one of the exercises provided, so you were able to have increased Gut Intelligence™ (GQ) before you decided. And of course, your decisions would consider what your gut, heart, head—and intuition—all told you is right for you!

But now that you have your plan, it's time to awaken to your intuition on a daily basis. All plans are meant to simply be a compass to guide you in a direction. But, if you go in that direction and you begin to see cues at the tip of the iceberg that tell you that your plan is not working, you need to pivot. Gut Intelligence™ (GQ) is the intelligence that will help you do so.

Now that you are doing the 5 Practices to Elevate your Consciousness daily, you can tap into your intuition and avoid the emotional reaction center of your brain. As a result of the gut-brain axis you've developed, you trust that ping in your gut to alert you when something is off. So, instead of doubting yourself, you *'Own it!'*

When you *'Own it!'*, that gut-alert, you can then get curious to discover why something felt off to you. Usually something feels off because the facts do not add up. I call this 'incongruency'.

When there is incongruency, we know it because what we hear is not the same as what we see, feel and experience! Below are some examples of how we pick up incongruencies:

- Someone says they are doing fine; but their body language and tone say otherwise.
- Someone says, "I will TRY to get that done", and we notice the word "try", and their body language and tone of voice do not sound enthusiastic.
- Someone is regularly late on projects, yet they say they are "doing their best".
- Someone tells you, "Your job is secure", but you see signs that the company is cutting expenses, people are getting laid off and clients are leaving.

These are just a few examples of how your intuition may pick up incongruent messages. When you pick up these incongruencies, you are exercising your Gut Intelligence™ (GQ). This will lead you to an intuitive knowing that can put the pieces of the puzzle together for you so you will just know. It is an intelligence that is much like the scientific process. It begins with a hypothesis and then that hypothesis is tested before conclusions and decisions are made. That is why intuition, when used correctly, is not 'emotional' or 'woo-woo' like some may label it.

When you effectively listen to your gut to alert you; your heart to align you to your vision, values and goals; and your head to assimilate the observations and information—you will begin to form your hypothesis. Then, you can raise your level of consciousness to gather more data to support this hypothesis. This includes asking your intuition to guide you to the information you need, like I did with my dad's blood type.

Your intuition will help you discover the information you need, when you become more open, trusting, and allowing of it to help you.

We do this by asking an open-ended question that begins with:

"How might I...?"

This question might be, "How might I find the information I need to conclude my hunch is correct?"

It's amazing when we ask an open-ended question like this, how our intuition will speak to us. I know we all have had that happen to us. Here are just a few examples, my clients have shared, of how this question led them to what they needed:

- They couldn't figure out where they left their cell phone, but then they took a deep breath, quieted their mind, asked their intuition, "How might I find my iPhone?" and they saw in their mind's eye where they left it.
- They felt stuck at work, and didn't know how to get to the next level, so they meditated and asked their intuition, "How might I get to the next level?" Suddenly they saw an article that gave them an idea, so they acted on their inspiration and got a new position.
- They almost hired a candidate because their resume looked great, but something felt off. When they asked their intuition what it was, they saw cues about their personality and lifestyle that told them that this candidate was not a culture fit.
- They couldn't figure out why the numbers weren't adding up on the Profit & Loss Statement. They paused, asked their intuition, "How might I find the missing piece?" ---and there it was!

These are just a few examples of how increased GQ can help you make effective decisions. Of course, the more you practice the 5 Levels of

Consciousness, and the corresponding practices in the previous chapters, the more quickly you will get your answer. This is because you will have strengthened your gut-brain axis and, therefore, will have awakened your intuition. And again, these skills can just as easily be applied in your personal life.

Your intuition knows you and your vision, values, and goals. Don't forget: You already mapped that all out, so now your intuition can synthesize the conscious and unconscious information to help you have that 'a-ha' knowing—a heightened awareness that puts the pieces of the puzzle together for you—and you just know!

The **Johari window**, helps to explain how this phenomenon works:

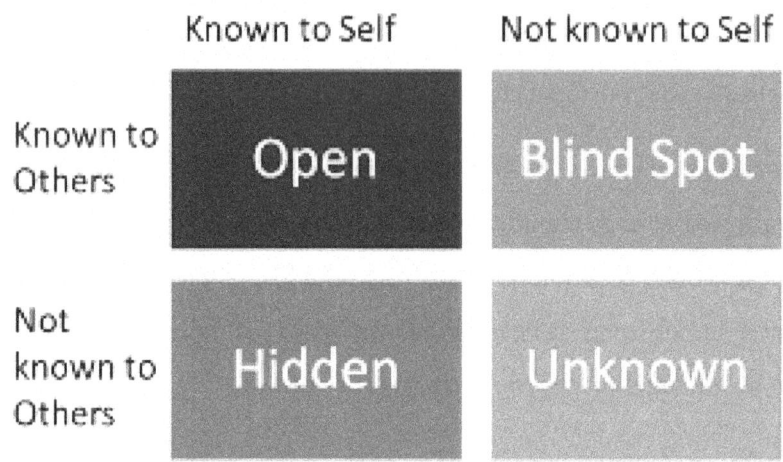

When you increase your Gut Intelligence (GQ), you engage your gut, heart, and head in decision-making. Then, when you invite your intuition into your decision-making by asking, "How might I...?", your intuition helps you see your Blind Spot and the Unknown. It is your Blind Spot and the Unknown that makes you fear you are making the wrong decision. But your intuition will help you know what you need to know in these two areas.

Let me illustrate how your intuition works with this story. Imagine you are driving down the highway at 100 miles an hour because you have someone in the car who is about to have a baby. Likely you would be focused on one thing: Get them to the hospital fast and safe. Now, imagine you drove down the expressway and passed your employee who was driving in the car with the owner of your company's biggest competitor. Your mind may have caught a glimpse of that scene, but you didn't fully register it because you were so focused on your immediate task.

Now, the mom and baby got to the hospital safe and sound. It is now Monday and you are back at work. But something seems odd to you. The employee who was in the car with your competitor has now called into work and said they were sick. You have a hunch something is up and ask your intuition, "How might I know what is going on with this employee?" Your intuition reminds you of that scene with him in the car with your competitor, that you almost forgot about. In addition, your intuition tells you to do the following: "Check his Facebook page and you will know."

So, you do what your intuition prompted you to do: You check his Facebook page and find out that the competitor is married to his cousin and they were on their way to a wedding. You know this from seeing their family and friends in wedding pictures that were just posted on Facebook. Still, while a bit relieved he was not on a job interview, you still wonder if this family tie could lead to your employee leaving the company. So, you ask your intuition, "How might I deal with this newfound information so that I can know if this employee is committed to us or them?"

You hear your intuition tell you, "Tell him the truth—that you saw him in the car with the competitor. Ask him what that is all about. When he tells you it's a relative, ask him if he is committed to your company or to his cousin's husband's company success?" You know that to stay intuitive, you need to be present when your employee is answering you. This means you need to listen to his words, but also his tone of voice, emotional energy, and body language. If anything feels incongruent—you will trust your GQ.

As you can see, when you *'Ask it!'*, your intuition will guide you the whole way on what to do and say. In this example, there was a Blind Spot on what the scene in the car meant. Even after checking on Facebook, there was still a bit of an Unknown. But when you follow intuition's guidance on what to do and say, you will discover what is going on in those Blind Spots and Unknown pieces of information.

Another way intuition guides us is seen through this Root Cause Diagram on the next page.

Root Cause Diagram

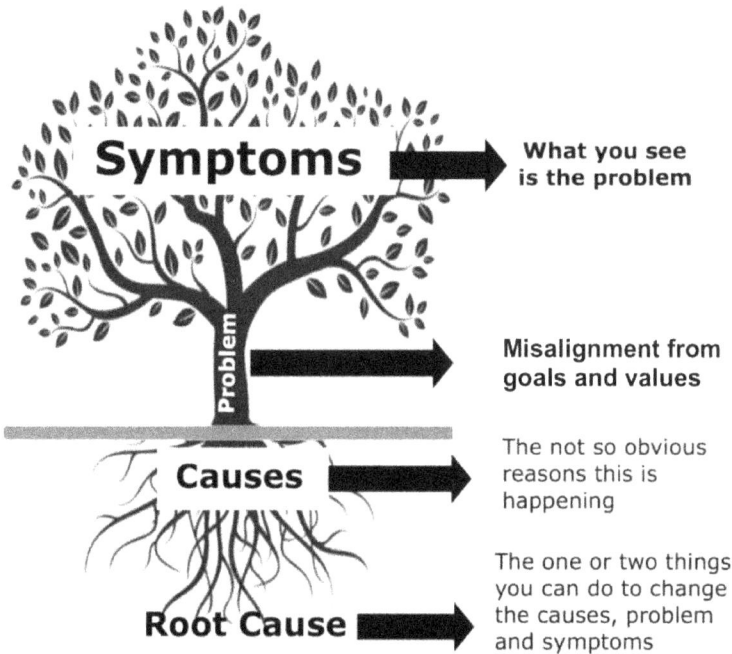

Symptoms → What you see is the problem

→ Misalignment from goals and values

Causes → The not so obvious reasons this is happening

Root Cause → The one or two things you can do to change the causes, problem and symptoms

Often, we don't realize there is a problem until we see symptoms that we don't like. These are the obvious things like: Someone is not meeting deadlines or following through; and it has caused a problem with our team and customer service. Notice there are symptoms and problems. This is the obvious thing that is going on and the thing most people complain about at work.

The Intuitive Leader, however, does not wait until the symptoms and the problem become so obvious. The Intuitive Leader already senses when there are causes taking root beneath the surface. For example, the Intuitive Leader would already notice if the resource allocation did not match the demand and therefore would intuit how the deadlines would be missed, and customers would become unhappy—even before this problem occurred. This means they would *'Voice it!'*, to create alignment between resources and projects before there was a problem, perhaps by outsourcing when needed.

In a situation like this, it would not only take intuitive wisdom to make that deduction; it would also take the guts to do something about it. Keep in mind: If you still have not reconciled and healed your belief that you are 'not capable or lovable enough'—you may fear speaking up in this very moment of opportunity to make things better. This may mean speaking up and allocating funds to needed resources, based on the workflow and sales projections. This is where we must be willing to take a risk because we can intuit the root cause that would avoid future problems and better align us to the goals. The risk may also be stepping on someone's toes because this change may reflect someone's unawareness and, therefore, threaten someone's job security because they weren't paying attention.

On the rare occasion, when the root cause is missed prior to the problem and symptoms, the Intuitive Leader does not focus on the symptoms, like most people do. They dig deeper, beyond the symptoms, to understand:

- What problems are these symptoms causing the organization?

- What are the root causes that are leading to these problems and symptoms?
- And what is the one or two root causes that will solve the above?

Of course, the leader with high Gut Intelligence™ (GQ) would catch the root causes because they would notice the incongruencies, even before it became a problem.

Keep in mind, this Gut Intelligence™ (GQ) decision-making process, can be utilized at home, as well as work. Generally speaking, big problems at home do not just happen overnight. Just as it is at work, there is a root cause growing beneath the surface before the big problems occur. When you use your GQ at home too, you will often solve the root cause before bigger problems occur.

I'm sure by now you can understand why GQ is as important as IQ and EQ. When we own that gut-alert that tells us to pay attention, and ask our intuition a, "How might I…?" question—we get the information we need to succeed. This helps us to become mindful of what is underground, in our Blind Spot or in the Unknown, and is not as easily seen by others with lower GQ.

With increased GQ, you will then be the leader who leads by: Ready, Aim, Fire! This is opposed to the leaders who do not see the cues early on and then everything is a Fire! Fire! Fire! In the first case there is more time for collaboration, where in the last scenario there is not. Hence, another benefit for having a high GQ—as it creates a collaborative culture.

On the next page, you will find a worksheet to help you increase your Gut Intelligence™ (GQ), and engage your intuition, so you can: *'Own it!'*, *'Ask it!'* and *'Voice it!'* This will help you to raise your level of consciousness in each of your brains: Gut, heart, and head.

Practice:
Increase your Gut Intelligence (GQ): *Own it! Ask it! Voice it!*

Step 1: *'Own it!'*

When _____happened,

I had a gut-alert that told me I needed to pay attention to_____.

Step 2: *'Ask it!'* (your intuitive that wants to shift you to your highest self)

As a result, I engaged my intuition and asked, How might I_____? (What do you want to know?)

(Now, practice your breathing to quiet your mind, as you learned in the previous chapters: 3 breaths in your nose out your mouth at these 5 locations: top of chest, chest, top of gut, mid-gut, hips)

Then,

- Look up to the right side of your mind's eye: What do you see?
- Listen in your left ear, what do you hear?
- Look down in your gut, what do you know for sure?
- Listen in your left ear, what do you hear?
- Look up to the right side of your mind's eye, what do you see?

Step 3: *'Voice it!'*

What did your intuition tell you to say or do?_____

In summary: As you work to develop your Gut Intelligence™ (GQ), there will be times you need to consciously go back into the lower level of consciousness to do 'The Work' of clearing any residual fear and self-doubt that continues to block your Intuitive Inner Knowing. In the next chapter, you will learn why this is important, as well as how to do 'The Work'.

Chapter Six: "The Work"

As you have seen by now:

The level of consciousness you choose to operate from has nothing to do with what is going on in your life.

The level of consciousness you are in has everything to do with the belief and mindset you choose to hold. While you used to think it was 'what they did or said'; or 'what life has dealt you'—you now know that this is not true. Your ability to show up in your life in a clear, calm, and confident way has everything to do with your level of consciousness. When you are clear, calm, and confident—regardless of your circumstances—this means you have done 'The Work' to awaken to your Intuitive Alignment.

'The Work' happens when you accept that life is an 'inside out' job.

This means that anytime you are feeling afraid, judgmental, or want to control—it is because you are attached to a certain outcome you still use to define your worth. This also means that somewhere deep down inside, you still believe you are not enough. That is 'The Work' you are doing—to rid yourself of this negative and limited-belief that is not allowing your intuition to guide your life.

For example, if you still believe a certain lifestyle defines your worth, you will be operating at Level 2 consciousness: Self-Doubt and Judgment. This is because you judge yourself as not good enough, unless you have a certain lifestyle you believe will define your worth as good enough. If this is the case, you will strive and drive to get that lifestyle—completely ignoring the guidance of your intuition and what it is telling you is best for your vocational, financial, mental, emotional, physical, spiritual and relationship overall wellness. And when you think about it, how could you possibly make decisions out of integrity if there is such a strong attachment to the outcome. That is why doing 'The Work' is important in effective leadership.

For example, while you may have a relationship or job that does not fulfill you or align with your desires or talents—you may continue to be with that person or job just because you think it impresses others, or gives you the lifestyle you think you need to feel 'enough'. This means that you will do what it takes to keep that relationship or job intact, even if it means ignoring your intuition and not being true to yourself.

Traditionally, women have defined themselves through their relationships. That is why if someone considers them a 'witch', they may back down on their intuition and speaking their truth. Men, traditionally, have defined themselves from their work, so they will often do what it takes to get promoted, even if it means ignoring their intuition, so they are not seen as a 'wimp' who can't provide or protect their family and company. Of course, these gender differences are beginning to change, as both men and women are becoming the primary or equal breadwinners.

Unfortunately, both women and men, when attached to the outcome at work, do not align with their authentic vision, values, and goals. This is because they are trying so hard to be 'enough' and, therefore, controlled by fear-based thinking. As the world is changing with more women rising in executive positions, we now see women struggling at work too—as they fear taking a risk that might negatively affect a relationship or inhibit their career advancement.

As you practice the higher levels of consciousness, however, you begin to feel the difference when you make a decision that is based on fear; or one that is in alignment with your intuitive knowing. The benefit you get from doing 'The Work' is to be in Intuitive Alignment and a feeling of being clear, calm, and confident. This contrasts with that chattering voice inside that is your ego's fear—trying to push you to do things to be enough. With practice, however, you realize that listening to the guidance of your intuition has a far greater benefit than any outcome you could imagine you could get from listening to your ego. You know it's your ego's fear when you are trying to control a relationship or job security. This is especially detrimental if it means you would be out of alignment with your authentic vision, values, and goals—which is often the case.

When you abandon your true self, and get the outcomes you strive for, you will feel lonely and still believe you are not enough. This is because you are chasing a mirage: Hoping that the outcome will somehow heal your belief that you are not enough. However, if that outcome is not derived from inspired action, your intuition—it will never feel enough, or be enough, to fill that hole inside of you.

Often, we must chase a few illusions in our life before we decide to do 'The Work' of figuring out what fear and negative belief is driving us.

By doing 'The Work', we can begin to understand what is right for us. When I say, 'The Work', and 'figuring it out'—I don't mean analyzing it. I mean awakening to the unconscious negative belief and surrendering it, so that your intuition can heal this negative belief and guide you to where you authentically desire to go. When you don't listen to this intuitive knowing, because you are so attached to getting the outcome you want, you will feel like you cheated and abandoned yourself in some odd way. That's because you did.

I learned this lesson after I sold my million-dollar lake house a couple years ago. When I think back to when I bought it 15 years ago, there was a lot of ego involved. The kids had just gone to college and I was now an empty nester. If I'm honest, I was afraid to be alone. But instead of dealing with that fear, I was unconscious and told myself, "This was my time!" This took a mid-life crisis to drive me to buy a 5,000 square-foot lake home, hoping it would keep the kids coming back and would fill my empty hole inside, in the meantime while they were gone.

Just typing this makes me a bit sick to my stomach, as I can feel how I felt like I was not lovable enough for them to come visit me if I had chosen to downsize then, like everyone advised! But, while that may not sound all that terrible to you, the year I bought the house it was at the top of the market. Even though everyone, including my intuition, told me it was not a great time to buy…I bought it anyway.

What happened? Of course, the next year the housing market crashed because of the recession we were all in. Many of my neighbors started to foreclose on their houses and the values of the properties went way down. Suddenly my house was worth 15% less than what I had into it. To ride out the storm, I stayed in the house for 13 years, until I could finally get close to the amount, I paid for it.

While I still lost some of my initial investment, the experience taught me what happens when we don't live in Intuitive Alignment: We get to instead do 'The Work'. 'The Work' allows us to see hindsight in 20/20. It's an opportunity to get conscious, where we were once operating at the level of unconsciousness. While it's difficult to admit that my intuition was trying to tell me not to buy the house all along, my unconscious fear of being an empty nester made me ignore the cues at the tip of the iceberg that said "Don't do it!"

I know I am not alone in this story. We are all here to learn and do 'The Work' to unfold into our higher consciousness. Maybe you didn't buy a lake house when your kids went to college, in hope they would frequently come back to visit you, but I am sure you made plenty of decisions from your unconscious belief that you were not enough. We all do that! And, when we do, we are given the opportunity to do 'The Work', to become conscious of the fear and negative belief that drove us to those decisions. When we awaken to these negative fears and beliefs, we become free to choose differently in the future, with the help of our intuitive guidance.

Doing 'The Work' gives us freedom from the fears and negative beliefs that drive us into choices that we believe we must have to be enough. This could mean a: house, car, job, title, lifestyle, relationship, body, clothes, religion, or company we associate with—or group of people we call 'friends', 'family' or 'community'.

It's amazing what happens when you do 'The Work' to let go of your fear of not being enough. Your chattering mind subsides, and your Intuitive Inner Voice takes front and center stage. There is no longer a separation of 'My Will' or 'Thine Will'. If this separation is still evident in you, that is because you are still struggling in the lower levels of consciousness where your fear is causing your attachment to an outcome. As you do 'The Work' to get to level 4 consciousness, Detachment, your Intuitive Inner Voice will become front and center.

Now, you can hear your intuition tell you what it is you are called to say or do in each moment. It's not as though you arrive at knowing your purpose—it's that you start becoming who you truly are meant to be. As you become more open, trusting, and allowing of your intuition to guide you in each moment, your purpose becomes clear.

Many people come to me hoping I can figure their purpose out for them. I tell them that the answer will come to them as we do 'The Work' to raise their level of consciousness. 'The Work' will help them discover the negative fears and beliefs that were driving them away from their Intuitive Inner Voice—who has the answer. While they often say they are ready to do 'The Work' to discover their true voice and purpose, they soon begin to realize that doing 'The Work' means identifying and giving up the addictions, distractions, people-pleasing behavior and attachments that kept them from Intuitive Alignment. This is a dance between your ego and essence that can often feel a lot like the cha-cha or the tango, instead of a smooth waltz.

Addictions, distractions, people-pleasing, and attachments can range from:

- Drinking too much or using drugs to escape.
- Living beyond your means to get a temporary feeling of being enough.
- Shopping to relieve yourself of boredom, loneliness, or any other uncomfortable feeling.
- Filling your life with material things.

- Partying to create a sense of "high".
- Busyness to create distraction.
- Becoming overly organized or rigid to create a sense of control.
- Spending time caretaking others; instead of caring for yourself.
- Creating dramas in your life, instead of making intuitive decisions that align to what you want to create.

These are just some ways we avoid doing 'The Work' to explore what we fear and why we don't believe we are enough.

Doing 'The Work' allows you to break through your fear, and regain an aspect of yourself, that once lost its expression.

You may, like me, have been more comfortable leading with a certain aspect of yourself that you deemed 'acceptable'. But maybe like me, you over-did that part of yourself, while suppressing another aspect.

I see this happen to my women clients all the time. For example, they may have a natural gift of nurturing and empathy. That is a great gift! Because they may have been validated for that gift, they may over-extend themselves in that way because it is a safe and acceptable expression of themselves. This can happen with men too who have been validated for providing for their families, and now overwork to continue to get that validation. But what if you took a risk: What part of yourself would you express, instead of suppressing that aspect of you?

Usually this suppressed aspect of our self is something we deem as 'different' than societal gender norms and, therefore, not as acceptable. In psychology there is something called, 'Difference-Shame'. Shame arises when we believe we have something different about us that is a 'defect'. This is some aspect of our self that we are afraid to expose to others. We are afraid to expose this to others because we believe we will be judged. Often, we fear we will be judged because we are different. Perhaps this is because someone judged this aspect of you in the past. For women—it is generally expressing their strength and guts to do something about situations they see before others do. For men—it is often showing their wisdom and expressing it in a more vulnerable way.

Doing 'The Work' means you notice who judged you, and how you gave your power away to them, by disregarding this aspect of yourself.

This is what 'The Work' is all about: To figure out what that aspect of yourself is that you have suppressed because you are different and afraid of being judged. This is what makes you believe 'you are not enough'! When you no longer suppress that part of you, you will be free to do what you love and be who you are—regardless if people love you or not. It will also help you to break through your fear, so you can now hear your intuitive inner voice guide you. Can you imagine how this breakthrough will help you create the life you love and help you become an Intuitive Leader who is more effective?

When you do 'The Work' to become who you truly are—your mind stops chattering and you don't need the job, stuff or people to validate you any longer.

That's because you are living from the inside out, versus the outside in! Now that you have quieted your chattering mind because you did 'The Work', you can listen to your intuitive voice that wants to help you find those lost aspects of yourself. As you do, and you express yourself freely, you will realize that there are people who will love and accept you—just as you are!

Furthermore, when you are ready to do 'The Work', you will automatically let go of the drama and distractions that keep you from higher levels of consciousness. This means, while you may notice someone judges you for who you are, you simply just notice that without giving it much energy. Then, you simply choose to operate from your higher level of consciousness, your Intuitive Alignment. Notice how this choice allows you to let go of the clutter in your life. This includes the people, stuff, and busyness that do not align with who you are or what you genuinely want to create, at work and home.

This doesn't mean you do not accept differences! In fact, as you do "The Work" to accept how you are different, you more lovingly and openly accept the differences in others. But, as you do 'The Work', you become more discerning on what is a fit for you, and what is not.

Taking the time to do 'The Work', so you can connect to your intuition, requires you take at least 20-minutes a day to meditate.

It's amazing how many people say they don't have time for meditation. Sara Lazar, a neuroscientist at Massachusetts General Hospital and Harvard Medical School, was one of the first scientists to do a study to prove that when we meditate 20-minutes a day, we change our brain and create a better gut-brain axis. When we meditate 20-minutes a day, we train ourselves to breathe more deeply into our gut. This allows us to transmit the neurons, hormones, and neurotransmitters up the vagus nerve, through our heart, up to our head—to the executive functioning part of our brain. As we help the corpus callosum become more efficient, through deep breathing, we access higher brain thinking and our Intuitive Inner Voice. This is because we are bypassing the amygdala part of our brain, the emotional center, that used to get us stuck in our fear and negative beliefs.[12]

When you do 'The Work', and meditate for at least 20-minutes every day, you will become more clear, calm, and confident about what to do or say in each moment. This does not mean you will never get triggered again into lower levels of consciousness that make you feel that you are not enough. But when you reach the highest level of Intuitive Alignment, by doing 'The Work' of becoming who you are, you will eventually discover your purpose and passion.

After I sold my big lake house, and freed up a lot of money and time, I decided to spend even more time in meditation every day. This included getting up each morning and meditating for 45-minutes and doing some yoga. Because I did not have a big nut to crack every month on a mortgage, or have to pay those big property taxes, I became more discerning on what work I choose to do—and with whom. Breaking free from my fear of having to make a certain income to keep up my lifestyle, allowed me to be more Intuitively Aligned. This meant I:

- Stopped trying to be what others expected.
- Chose the work I wanted to do.
- Chose the people I wanted to work with.
- Did the work in the way that represented my authentic vision, values, and goals.
- Let go of the outcome, and more readily spoke my truth.
- Let go of the relationships and work that didn't align to my philosophy.
- Spent more time alone because I enjoyed my company more than anyone else's.
- Showed up more loving, and less stressful, because I took care of myself first.

When you do 'The Work' of awakening to your true self, through Intuitive Alignment, you also have less drama in your life.

Outward drama in one's life is a mirror to one's inner chaos.

Having drama, or a drama-free life, reflects the level of consciousness you are in. If you are in Level 1: Unconsciousness or Level 2: Self-Doubt and Judgment—you will have a lot of drama because you are not successfully listening to your intuition to solve your problems. But if you are in Level 3: Self-Awareness, you will realize when something is not working for you. Then, by detaching from the outcome, in Level 4, you can find your courage to realize what you genuinely want. Then, when you surrender your situation and what you want, in Level 5, you will intuitively know what to do or say to create the life you want, at work and home. No drama. Just do it, like Nike says. It's as simple as that.

As you can see, doing 'The Work' will help you to show up differently in your life, both at work and at home. This means you will become the leader in your life who is no longer submissive to other's expectations and control. By doing 'The Work', you develop your own personal leadership and, therefore, are ready to lead others in a different way. First you must do 'The Work' before you can lead others effectively. It is an inside-out job to break free from your fear first, so you can become Intuitively Aligned—then you can become an Intuitive Leader.

By acknowledging your own level of consciousness, you see where others are in their consciousness too. This helps you to be a better leader because you know when you are in your ego versus Intuitively Aligned. As a result, you can see the difference in others too. Because you understand what it takes to get yourself to higher levels of consciousness; you know what it takes to get others there as well.

The Speed of the Leader is the Speed of the Gang.

This is a saying I tell all the executives I coach. It explains how we cannot take others where we have not gone our self. This means that if you are a leader and operating at lower levels of consciousness, you will have chaos around you. I cannot tell you how many leaders have called me asking me to "fix their people." When I ask them if they are willing to do 'The Work' that begins with them, many opt out. Why? Because it is easier to see what's wrong with someone else, than it is to self-reflect.

That is why outer chaos is a mirror reflection of one's inner chaos that has not yet been explored and reconciled. If a leader is seeing chaos around them, for example, it would be beneficial for them to first look inside and ask themselves, "How might this chaos be a reflection of 'The Work' I need to do?" When you are a leader who leads from the inside-out, you will change your environment and relationships—by changing you first.

'The Work' requires you to look at your own fears and beliefs that make you think: You are not enough to get the results you desire.

Instead of reacting from your grandiose or insecure ego, like many leaders do, you can instead do 'The Work' to clear your fear and negative belief. By doing 'The Work' to break through your fear, you will consciously choose to re-visit the lower levels of consciousness again. This will allow you to examine your beliefs, thoughts, feelings, and behaviors that keep giving you that same ole same ole feeling—that you are not enough.

Did someone do or say something that you thought made you feel:

- Disrespected?
- Inadequate?
- Unloved?
- Unsafe?
- Insecure?
- Offended?
- Angry?
- Hurt?
- Sad?
- Not enough?

If so, you are experiencing The Velcro-Effect. This means go down to level 2 consciousness and do 'The Work' to own your own self-doubt and judgment, that you used to project on their communication and actions. Instead of projecting on them your self-doubt and judgment, ask yourself these questions: What if…

- The feeling of disrespect I thought was them; was me disrespecting myself because I am allowing their behavior?
- I believed it was them treating me or talking to me as though I was inadequate; but it was really me buying into that belief that I was not adequate?

- I believed they were treating me in an unlovable way; but it really was me who believed I was unlovable?
- I believed their behavior made me feel unsafe; but it was really me not trusting myself and doing what I needed to do or say on my behalf?
- I thought their behavior made me feel insecure; but I just felt insecure deep inside?
- I was not offended by them; but instead I just struggled with not being right or in control?
- They weren't making me feel angry; but my anger was telling me something needed to change?
- I didn't have to take their behavior personally; but could go deeper to understand The Velcro Effect and what negative belief in me their behavior stuck to?
- They didn't make me sad or disappointed; but I just had to face the truth and let go of some kind of expectation or outcome I was still attached to?

When you do "The Work", you take advantage of the lower levels of consciousness that arise, so you can awaken to the fears and negative beliefs that still tell you, "You are not enough". As you become self-aware, you awaken to a higher level of consciousness, where you have the choice to detach from these old ego-scripts that once controlled you. Doing 'The Work' helps you to no longer give your power away to others. Instead, you can ask yourself: Will I take the power back onto myself? Or will I continue to give it away to someone else?

Doing 'The Work', allows you to re-visit all your fears and negative beliefs that stand in the way of you becoming your potential.

To do 'The Work' you need to ask yourself these questions:

- When I simply notice other's expectations and choose to listen to my intuition instead, what am I afraid may happen?
- If that outcome does happen, how does that become a mirror reflection that 'I am not enough'?
- What am I afraid will happen if I transcend that fear of 'not being enough' and become my true and powerful self instead?

Realizing the answers to these three questions will help you do 'The Work' of removing any negative beliefs and fears that are getting in the way of your potential. By doing 'The Work', you will learn how to detach from your negative beliefs and fears that once kept you from:

- Owning your truth.
- Asking your intuition for guidance.
- Voicing your truth to others and following through with the guts to do something about it!

Now that you are free from your attachment to the outcome, you can allow your intuition to be at work in your life. However, if at any time you get triggered, you will be able to use this Elevator Meditation and The Elevator Meditation Worksheet that follows to do 'The Work', so you can awaken to your intuition once again.

Because leadership is an inside-out job—this will prepare you for the next chapter which will outline the 15 Characteristics of an Intuitive Leader.

The Elevator Meditation

When stuff happens, and you get triggered into lower levels of consciousness, do this Elevator Meditation, and the corresponding worksheet, to help you do 'The Work'. This Elevator Meditation will help you to clear your fear and any negative beliefs that are still telling you— you not enough! By taking the elevator down to the lower levels of consciousness, and doing 'The Work', you will get out of your sticky situation!

Here's how the Elevator Meditation works:

1) **Breathe 3 times**, in your nose and out your mouth, gradually and slowly at these points in your body: Upper chest, middle chest, upper diaphragm, middle diaphragm, lower gut, base of your tailbone.
2) **Now imagine yourself in an elevator. Press level one. This is The Basement.** Notice how dark and cold it is in The Basement. Take your cell phone out and turn the light on. Go walk to the right corner of The Basement. In the corner is something you need to see that's a reminder from your childhood (birth to eight years old). It is something that represents how you felt undeserving, not capable, or lovable enough. What is it? Take it to the elevator.
3) **In the elevator, press level 2: The Kitchen.** This is where your family cooked up a lot of negative stories that made you feel fear. Go sit at the kitchen table and listen to those negative stories and feel how they made you feel self-doubt and judgment. Who is at the table with you? How are the stories

telling you that you are not deserving, capable or lovable enough? Now, go back to the elevator.

4) **In the elevator, press level 3: The Closet.** When you get off the elevator you will walk into a huge closet—it is your closet and it is the whole floor. In the closet are all kinds of things that were put in there by other people for you to keep. These are things you just accepted, but do not really love. Notice what is in the closet that represents beliefs, expectations, and desires from others. Pick up the things you do not want and throw them in the garbage to your right. Throw out everything you do not want. Now, pick one thing you love that represents your authentic self. Notice it—why does this represent your authentic self? Now, bring it with you and go back to the elevator.

5) **In the elevator, press level 4: The Waiting Room**. In this room, there is a big comfy chair next to a table. Notice how the light is shining brightly on the table that has a big piece of poster board on it. Next to it are a box of crayons. Look at the item you brought from your closet and set it on the table. Now draw three images on the poster board that represents who you are and what is most important for you to create in your life. Let the item from your closet inspire you. When you are done, take your poster board, and go to the elevator.

6) **In the elevator, press level 5: The Rooftop.** At this level you can look down and see your life from the past, present and future. Look to the left and see your past. Notice what most affected you and defined you. Just notice it—not as good or bad—just as something that occurred. Detach from it, bless it, and take with you what you learned.

   Now, look in front of you. This is your present life. Again, just notice it and ask yourself, "What do I want to take with me in the future and what do I want to leave behind?" Now, look to the right: This is your future. This is what you want to create. Check in with your gut, heart, and head—are they all in agreement? Now, ask your intuition, "How might I get what I want in my future?' Check in visually, auditorily and in your gut. What do you know for sure?

The Elevator Meditation Worksheet

What came to you in your meditation at each floor of consciousness:

- **Level One: The Basement (Unconsciousness):** What item did you take from your childhood that reminded you of how you felt undeserving, not capable or not lovable enough? Why did it make you feel this way?

- **Level Two: The Kitchen (Self-doubt and Judgment):** What kind of stories were being cooked up in your family kitchen that led you to feel fear, self-doubt and judgment? How did these stories create self-doubt and judgment in you, such that you felt undeserving, not capable or lovable enough?

- **Level Three: The Closet (Self-Awareness):** What did you throw out of your closet? What beliefs and expectations did these things represent? What was the one item you kept that represented your authentic self? How did it represent your authentic self?

- **Level Four: The Waiting Room (Detachment):** What 3 images did you draw on your poster board? How were they inspired by the item you took from your closet? Now what do you know you want to create in your life as a result of this exercise?

- **Level Five: The Rooftop (Intuitive Alignment):**
  What did you see from your past that you let go of?

  What did you see in your present life that you want to let go of?

  What do you want to take with you into your future that is in your current life?

  What did you see in your future?

  Were your gut, heart, and head in agreement?

  What did your intuition tell you about how to create this life?

Chapter Seven: Become an Intuitive Leader

Now that you have done 'The Work' to elevate your consciousness, so you can be Intuitively Aligned, it's time to put what you learned in the previous chapters into practice so you can become an Intuitive Leader. An Intuitive Leader is anyone who is conscious of themselves, the people and circumstances around them, and the life they want to create—at work and home. Being an Intuitive Leader means you have increased your Gut Intelligence™ GQ, so you can show up in each moment to make effective decisions that are aligned to your vision, values, and goals. Being an Intuitive Leader is not a title, it's a way of being.

This means you will not 'Witch-out' or 'Wimp-out' at the first sight of conflict, difficulty, or an adversarial situation. Nope, that's not you! Instead you will use the techniques, discussed in the prior chapters, to increase your Gut Intelligence™ GQ.

Becoming an Intuitive Leader will not only help your company grow, it will help you grow into your true potential.

On the next page, you will find the 15 Characteristics of an Intuitive Leader. These characteristics will help you better understand what it means to apply what you have learned so far to your personal and professional life. Think of this acronym as a summary of everything you learned. When you use this acronym as a way of being. By practicing the 15 Characteristics of an Intuitive Leader, you will awaken to your potential. Memorize the acronym: INTUITIVE LEADER, on the following page so you can approach everyone and every situation with a higher level of consciousness.

Once you memorize the 15 Characteristics and their meaning, you can do a gut-check with yourself in the moments when you feel susceptible to your negative beliefs, fears, and attachments to the outcome. This could be caused by: Self-doubt, judgment, others who are defensive, critical of you, not following through, pushing back, disagreeing, or dismissing you. Sometimes it is caused by you being tired or over-worked; or not doing your 5 Practices to Elevate your Consciousness.

Instead of allowing someone else's behavior to Velcro your negative beliefs about yourself, just evaluate yourself by using the 15 Characteristics of an Intuitive Leader you will see on the next page. This will help you to become self-aware, so you can focus on improving the areas of your leadership that may need some tweaking. A few simple tweaks can help you become your greatest potential.

At first, you may find it helpful to rate yourself weekly on each characteristic until these characteristics become a habit. Then, you can eventually rate yourself monthly and quarterly. After you evaluate yourself on a regular basis, you will ingrain the habits of these 15 Characteristics of an Intuitive Leader. And, once these characteristics have become a habit, you will confidently be able to pull the acronym up in your mind for review. If you are a company leader, you may want to include this acronym in your performance reviews, as it will help your talent to understand what it means to be an Intuitive Leader, from the point of view of their job description.

Now, let's look at the acronym: INTUITIVE LEADER. After you see the acronym on the next page, you will get the full description on the following pages for each characteristic. Then, after the descriptions of each characteristic, you will see a survey to rate yourself on how well you do with each characteristic. In addition, you will also get a total score with some suggestions for becoming a better Intuitive Leader.

15 Characteristics of an Intuitive Leader:

___**I**-*Introspective*

___**N**-*Non-Judgmental*

___**T**-*Truthful*

___**U**-*Undaunted*

___**I**-*Instinctive*

___**T**-*Trusting*

___**I**-*Integrated*

___**V**-*Visionary*

___**E**-*Engaging*

___**L**-*Love*

___**E**-*Exploratory*

___**A**-*Accountability*

___**D**-*Determined*

___**E**-*Essence*

___**R**-*Risk-taking*

I-*Introspective:*
Spends time examining your own beliefs, thoughts, feelings, and behavior and the impact to results.

You stop giving your power away to others when you turn inward to face your fears and the hidden beliefs within that keep you from trusting yourself and your intuition. Being introspective reminds you to take personal responsibility before you look to someone else to blame.

Being introspective means you first look at what beliefs, thoughts, and feelings are driving your behavior. This contrasts with blaming others for how you feel. When you are introspective, you check out your beliefs, thoughts, and feelings and how you are reacting to others; versus responding in alignment with what it is you want to create.

The Introspective Exercise below will help you with self-reflection. Do this exercise whenever you feel you are in a sticky situation. Perhaps you are experiencing The Velcro Effect and need a bit more insight. This exercise will take you through your beliefs, thoughts, feelings, and behavior so you can go to level 3 consciousness and become more self-aware.

Introspective Exercise

What is bothering me? Fill in this blank:

When _____happened,

I felt _____ because I believed _____.

My own reaction towards this tends to be:

- To blame myself and tell myself (I'm not deserving, capable or lovable enough)?

- To blame others by judging them as (not deserving, capable or lovable enough?)

- To go into a fight pattern by trying to control the outcome so I can get …?

- To flee from my truth because I believe if I speak it this consequence will happen?

- What negative belief am I still holding, that tells me I am not deserving, capable or lovable enough?

Now, detach from that fear and negative belief and ask your intuition, "How might I best deal with this situation to effectively align to my vision, values and goals?

N-*Non-Judgmental:*
An unbiased observer who accepts differences without needing to decide who is right or wrong.

When you quickly judge someone, you are missing an opportunity to be empathetic. Being empathetic means looking deeper beneath the surface to understand 'why' someone is choosing the behavior that they are choosing. This means being curious to discover the 'root cause' behind their behavior and choice. This allows you to stop and consider the reason behind someone's choices. In addition, it will stop you from projecting your own fear and insecurity onto them.

Being non-judgmental helps you be a more effective leader in many ways. Instead of barking out orders to try to control people, you stop to understand people. This doesn't mean you sympathize with them, which would cause you to enable their behavior. It just means you look more deeply to realize their reasons and circumstances, from their perspective.

By not being judgmental, you also neutralize your emotions you would otherwise have if you were judgmental. Being non-judgmental also makes you a better problem-solver because you become objective and focus on solving the problem, instead of blaming the person.

.

Non-judgment Exercise

Write down your judgmental thoughts below, and then re-frame them by getting into a curious mindset. Notice how this judgment was covering a deeper fear or belief you had. Look at it and ask yourself what you want to do about that fear. Then, get more curious about where the other person is coming from, so you can discover the root cause and need.

1) What was my initial judgment towards this person?

2) How does their behavior affect me and what I want?

3) How does my judgment cover up a deeper fear or belief that might have?

4) What might their behavior be revealing about their own fears and beliefs?

5) What do I need to ask them to better understand their behavior?

T-_Truth, in Love_
One that always speaks in a straightforward way, with the intention of creating good and growth.

Within each of us is a Board of Directors desiring to guide us to speak the truth, in love. This means that when we get to the 5th level of consciousness, we are listening to our gut, heart and head that are all connected so that we are able to hear our Intuitive Inner Voice speak to us. This allows us to speak our truth, in love, for the good of all. When we speak our truth, in love, it is not because we are trying to control the outcome. It is because we are calling each other out to be our best selves and to be in alignment with the agreed upon vision, values, and goals.

Say for example, someone is abrupt with you and you don't like it. What do you do? Do you speak your truth, in love, and say to them, "I am feeling a bit rushed right now. I'd like to slow this down a bit so I have room to digest what we are discussing and, therefore, can consider my thoughts..." Note how you just stated what you felt and then what you needed. This contrasts with reacting unconsciously in a flight or fight manner that would either avoid the conversation or say, "You are rushing me!"

Keep in mind you only react when your gut, heart, and head are out of alignment. You will always get a ping in the gut that tells you when you need to pay attention. But if you perceive a negative outcome when you consider speaking your truth, your gut will send a signal to the amygdala that you are in danger and you will react—as if a bear is chasing you! This automatically sends you into black and white thinking: Fight or flight. That's what makes you sound like 'The Witch', the 'Arrogant Jerk', or the 'Wimp'.

When you communicate with people in an aggressive (fight) or passive (flight) way, you can be sure you are operating at the lower levels of consciousness and, therefore, not speaking your truth, in love. Sure, you are communicating, but you are communicating with the consciousness of fear, judgment, and control; instead of being open, trusting and allowing your intuition to speak through you.

Truth, in love, Exercise

1) Before you speak, ask yourself how speaking up will enhance growth, so that you have a positive focused intention. Write your answer below:

2) Finish this sentence:
   I am feeling
   _____

   What I need is
   _____

U-*Undaunted*
Not intimidated or discouraged by difficulty, danger, or disappointment.

As an Intuitive Leader, both in your personal and professional life, you will be taking risks to speak up and take action at the tip of the iceberg. Sometimes it will not go as expected! Instead of getting caught up in the lower levels of consciousness, like self-doubt and judgment, you will be undismayed and not abandon your purpose or vision, values, and goals.

This does not mean you will dig in your heels on your position. This means you will continue to allow for the unfoldment of information and ideas to fully align you to your vision, values, and goals. In fact, you don't care if your original idea is taken or not, you care about results and, therefore, will not give in to fear or unlimited thinking. You are unwavering with your focus on, "How might we reach the vision, values and goals?". You are also open, trusting and allowing your intuition to show you 'how'.

To continue in your courageous journey to your vision, values, and goals—do the following fishbone exercise below. It will help you understand how to discern between problems, symptoms and what is truly the root cause and need. Allow for the discovery and the unfoldment, as you are a leader who is undaunted!

To do the Fishbone Diagram start with putting the problems on the thicker bones that are extended from the fish. Then, on the thinner bones that project from that problem-bones, put all the symptoms you see to support that problem. Now that you see all the problems and the symptoms, ask your intuition, "What is the root cause and need?" Do one of the meditations from this book to help you quiet your mind and get clear. Then, after you hear your intuition guide you, put your answer in the fishbone's head. There it is—this is your root cause and need!

Fishbone Diagram

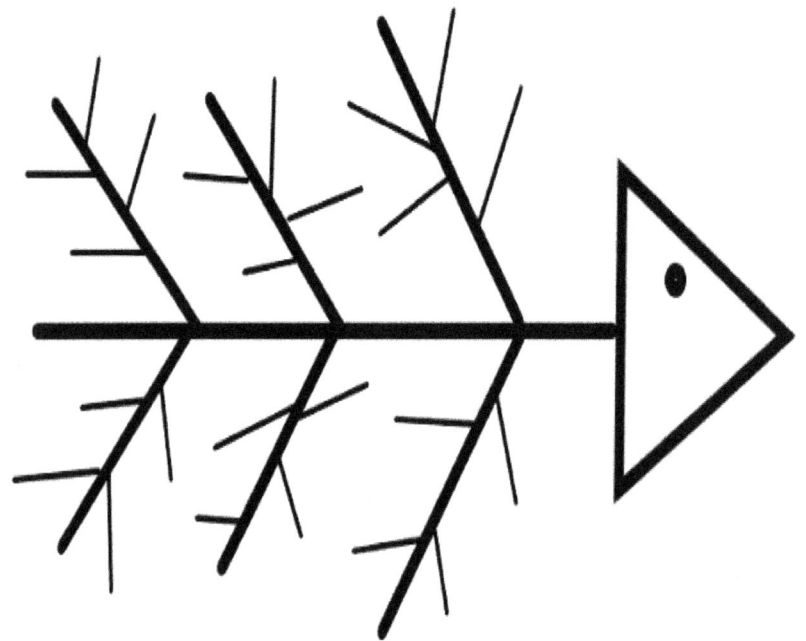

I-*Instinctive*
Trusting in something you know,
rather than something you have been taught.

Sometimes we know things automatically. When we have increased our Gut Intelligence™ (GQ) and are operating at Level 5 consciousness, our intuition speaks to us and points things out. We get prompted to pay attention by that gut-alert. We also have created a superhighway between the gut, heart, and head so that we quickly synthesize information unconsciously and consciously.

The Intuitive Leader is grateful for this Board of Directors within to guide them. Trust in your prior experience and your Gut Intelligence™ (GQ) to guide you personally and professionally. When your instinct is leading you, but you are having a difficult time trusting, do the following exercise below to raise your level of awareness so you can articulate your instinct to others

Instinct Exercise

1) What was brought to my attention, instinctively (my gut-alert)?

2) What prior experience is helping me with this instinct?

3) What does my Gut Intelligence™ (GQ) say about this situation?
   - Gut:

   - Heart:

- Head:

- Intuition:

T-_Trusting_
A firm belief in the strength of your Intuitive Inner Voice to guide you and help you manifest.

Your mind is so powerful. Most of us only use a fraction of what our mind can do for us because we are operating at a lower level of consciousness. When you get beyond your lower levels of consciousness, your black and white thinking, you can see the possibilities that exist to get you what you want most.

Seeing what you want in your mind's eye, even before it manifests, helps you to manifest it. This is The Heisenberg Theory at work, which we discussed in the previous chapters. When you are operating at a high level of trust, you are seeing things as you want them to unfold; not as you fear they might unfold. This does not mean you are in denial and not paying attention to the cues at the tip of the iceberg. This means that you are not allowing your fear to make you go into reaction. You are asking, believing and receiving—because you are trusting.

When you notice what is, you simply observe—trusting that it will unfold in alignment with your vision, values, and goals. As you observe it—and step into it with trust and intention—what you observe will shift. This means that if you observe that a gap appears between what is happening and what you imagine in your mind's eye—you can simply first imagine your higher consciousness helping you to make the shift you desire. This requires trust in your intuition to guide you where you and others need to go, even before you say or do anything. This helps to soften the other person to respond to you, instead of to react.

Instead of going to the lower level consciousness of self-doubt and judgment, you awaken to your Intuitive Alignment and become more open, trusting, and allowing of your higher consciousness to help you. Practice the Heisenberg Theory Exercise below to improve your trust and Intuitive Alignment.

The Heisenberg Theory

1) What do you need to observe?
   _____

2) What do you want shifted?
   _____

3) Imagine it is as you wish: See it, feel it, experience it with all your senses.

4) What is your intuition telling you that you need to do or say to get your vision and intention?

I-*Integrated*
The process of synching the gut, heart, and head through deep breathing, and higher consciousness, so that you can transcend fear and hear your Intuitive Inner Voice.

If you get so busy that you believe you do not have enough time to meditate or breathe deeply, you can be assured that you are in the lower levels of consciousness again. This means your ego has taken over and you are either being so grandiose that you think, "If it's meant to be, it's up to me!" or you believe, "I am not enough to make this happen, so I have to strive and drive!"

When you get back into that mindset, you are no longer integrated with your gut, heart, head, and intuition. Don't forget that when you are integrated, you are operating out of the executive functioning part of your brain. But when you are not, you are operating out of the amygdala—the emotional center of fight and flight.

Likely an unconscious fear and belief is driving you if you are not integrated. If this is the case, do the exercise below so you can become integrated again.

Integration Exercise

1) Do you find yourself currently:
   - Striving and driving to be enough?

   - Believing, "If it's meant to be it's up to me!"

2) What are you afraid might happen if you became more open, trusting and allowing others to do it in their way? How might you trust your intuition to guide you to cues if things start to get off track?

3) How might you find a time you can meditate, 20-minutes a day, to get integrated again?

V-_Visionary_
Thinking and planning the future with imagination, wisdom, and intuition.

Children are great at play and imagination. Sometimes as adults, we lose this gift. We spend so much time in front of our computer and in Zoom meetings, that we don't allow enough time to just imagine the future.

As a leader, you need to be the visionary who ingrains this image in people's minds, so they understand the 'why' they are doing what they are doing. Seeing the vision, allows the day-to-day tasks to become more meaningful. Even after you have set the vision, you need to revisit the vision often, and tie the goals, projects, and tasks to the vision.

By continually operating at the 10,000-foot level as a visionary leader, you give meaning to what otherwise could be the mundane. Do the Visionary Meeting Exercise below at all of your meetings to remind people of the Vision.

Visionary Meeting Agenda

Vision:_____
Goal we need to focus on:_____
Project we need to focus on:_____
Why this project is important to the goal and vision:

What values and standards we need to uphold on this project?

Topic for Discussion:
"How might we focus our project and tasks to meet the vision and goals?"

Agreed Upon Tasks and Standards:

What   Who   What is the Standard   When Completed   Why needed

1)

2)

3)

4)

5)

E-*Engaging*
To be curious about the beliefs, thoughts, feelings, and ideas of others in order to achieve the vision, values and goals.

As you can see in the meeting exercise above, when we engage others in the vision, values, goals, and needed projects and tasks to achieve our vision, we create a synergistic team. Notice how that outline allows for this alignment and conversation.

Engaging leaders not only use this meeting format, they use the 'Ask-lead' style of leadership instead of 'Tell-lead'. When you ask others the following questions, you engage them:

Use the following Engagement questions to 'Ask-lead' and engage your team.

Engagement Conversation

- What goal do you think we need to focus on to meet the vision?

- What projects do you think will help us meet the goals?

- What are the values and standards we need to uphold in this project?

- What tasks need to get done to finish the project?
    - Who will do what by when?

    - What standards do we expect for each task?

By 'Ask-leading' instead of 'Tell-leading' you get more engagement and buy-in. The McKinsey Study says that leaders who engage in this way get up to 74% more productivity. Use the Visionary Meeting Agenda, on the prior page to record your findings and agreed upon tasks and standards.

L-*Love*-
Leading with love means to let go of fear so you can lead with your vision, values, and goals and the question, "How might we…?".

When we lead with our vision, our visionary meeting agenda, and our "Ask-lead" style of leadership, we still may be met with resistance. Resistance occurs when someone feels fear that they are not enough to meet the expectations or when they have judgment about the direction.

Instead of reacting to this resistance, with your own fear, respond in love. Responding in love means you are compassionate with them because you understand that their resistance comes from fear. Instead of allowing it to create fear in you, simply focus on what you love—the vision, values, and goals of your company! Because you are focused on what you love and what you want to create, you lead them out of their fear into the love of the vision.

To lead from love, instead of fear when you see resistance, do the following exercise:

Tai Chi Resistance Exercise

When someone comes at you with resistance, it's natural to want to give them a karate chop back. This is because you have been triggered into your ego's mindset of: fear, judgment, and control. To resist getting into a power and control struggle, use your mind to do the following Tai Chi Exercise: Observe the resistance and then focus on what you want to create. This is another exercise in The Heisenberg Theory:

1) When someone is creating resistance, just imagine it going past you and observe it. Flow with the movement as though it is wind just blowing past you.

2) Now, stand tall like an oak tree and stand in your truth about your vision, values, and goals. What is your truth? Observe it.

3) Now, don't say anything, but look at the other person and smile. Soften your heart and any resistance you feel in your body. Let any fear go as though it is just dropping away from both of you, like a dead leaf falling off a tree.

4) Now, look at the other person, with a soft and curious mindset, and ask yourself, "I wonder, 'How might we get past this resistance'?" Just stay in an open, trusting, and allowing mindset and see how intuition guides you both past resistance

E-*Exploratory*
***To wonder about what to do or say with a "How might we…?"
question that sparks conversation and aligns everyone to
the vision, values, and goals.***

By becoming open, trusting, and allowing intuition to lead—you create an exploratory conversation that honors the intuition in you and others. This exploration helps everyone to get past resistance because they start to see the possibilities.

Exploring possibilities, without judgment, is fun! It allows us to have an open mindset where all things are possible. Even if you begin to not see things the same way, when you stay open-minded, you eventually see a possibility that takes you to the 'Grey Matter'. The 'Grey Matter' is an answer that considers 'this and that'.

To be an Intuitive Leader who allows for exploratory conversation, do the following Exploratory Exercise:

Exploratory Exercise

1) Name what you are solving: "How might we…(what)?"

2) Brainstorm: List all the possibilities that might work, without judgment. Continue the list, and write them down, without comment. Keep saying, "What else?" to exhaust all possibilities.

3) Narrow it down: Circle everything you both agree could work.

4) Narrow it down further: Now pick your top two ideas and share why you think those are best so you can understand the value-system behind the decision.

5) See if you have one idea in common and if your value-system aligns.

6) Tweak where necessary.

7) Choose a decision and benchmark the progress in 7-14 days.

8) Tweak again where necessary when you meet to benchmark.

A-*Accountability*
A willingness to accept responsibility for one's actions.

Oftentimes leaders 'Tell-lead' and get an attitude like Nike and say to their talent, "Just do it!" But in business, this seems to always fail long-term. Why? Because there is no engagement or buy-in. It doesn't even matter if your intuition is right: No one likes to be told what to do.

Other times you will have an exploratory conversation, and someone will just not follow through. Of course, they will tell you all kinds of excuses. If you buy-into those excuses and play Ms. or Mr. Nice, it would be because you are back in your 'Witch Complex', 'Arrogant Jerk Complex' or 'Wimp Complex'. If that's the case, you missed an opportunity for leading with accountability. Holding people accountable does not make you a 'Witch' or 'Arrogant jerk'! It makes you a leader who expects someone's word to be their honor.

To help you with accountability, do the exercise below:

Accountability Conversation:

Problem-solving Statement:

1) Don't you agree that we had agreed to the following: _____?
   (Name what you agreed to prior)

Get Curious: Seek to Understand First:

2) What was your understanding of our agreement?

3) What could you have done differently to uphold that agreement?

Share Your Truth, in Love:

4) Here is my viewpoint of the opportunities you missed to following through with your commitment:
   _____

5) Here is what I expect in the future:

Resolve:

6) Based on our conversation, how might you ensure you follow-through in the future?

D-*Determined*
An unwavering intention to find the possibilities to accomplish something.

When you are unwavering and determined, you will keep your focus on achieving the vision, values, and goals. If your mindset goes back to your fears and beliefs that it is not okay to be powerful, then just notice that. It is just your conditioning and fear that tells you that being determined somehow makes you a 'Witch' or an 'Arrogant jerk'. When you are Intuitively Aligned, and determined, you won't come across that way to others.

When that fear arises, however, remind yourself that your job is not to be liked! Your job is to help people be their potential so they can get past their own resistance. When you help people to overcome resistance, they will accomplish their goals. And, eventually, they will thank you for how you were determined, and how you helped them be determined too.

Research tells us that when we meet our goals, we raise our self-esteem. Being determined, and helping others to do the same, will make you a great leader in your personal and professional life. To help you stay determined, do the following exercise:

Determination Exercise

Watch the Apollo 13 movie. Notice how the leader tells his people, *"Work the problem folks. Failure is not an option!"* When his staff is telling him what they can't do, he meets their resistance with determination, by telling them, *"Don't tell me what you can't do. Tell me what you can do!"*

Strong determination leads others to figure out possible ways to find a solution within the parameters they have. It also teaches others how to get out of their fear and limited thinking so they can allow their intuitive minds to show them a possibility they otherwise would not realize. Use the questions below to realize where you need to express more determination.

1) Where are you finding resistance?

2) To whom do you need to say, "Work the problem—tell me what you can do!"

3) Now use the Exploratory Exercise we did earlier to have a productive conversation that is focused on possibilities, so everyone is determined to find a solution.

E-*Essence*
To act from your real nature so you can be continually Intuitively Aligned.

No matter how conscious you may have become, you will get your ego triggered from time to time. This means you will be back in your fear—threatened at some level.

When this occurs, you will lose your Intuitive Alignment and will want to operate from your ego: That reaction to self-protect which is fight or flight.

The key is to have a mantra to quickly get you back to your Essence, that Intuitive Alignment once again. To quickly raise your level of consciousness, and reconnect with your Essence, do the following Essence Exercise:

Essence Exercise

Ask yourself the following questions, and do the following mantras, to get yourself quickly back on track to your Intuitive Alignment:

- Say: It is what it is! (Use the space below to neutralize the storyline you are telling yourself);

- Ask yourself: What outcome feels threatened for me because of what I am observing?

- Now, the question becomes, "How might I deal with this threat so I can get all parties aligned to the vision, values, and goals?"

- What is my intuition telling me to do or say to assert myself and this alignment?

R-*Risk-taking*
The act of doing something that is not guaranteed as safe and is out of the ordinary, therefore, could create a degree of possible loss.

Women are not known for taking risks. But this is not because women are biologically risk averse. It is a learned behavior; thus, it can be unlearned. Learning to take risks is necessary to become an effective leader. The key is to listen to your Gut Intelligence™ (GQ) that is giving you the wisdom to know the truth and the guts to do something about it.

How do we get the guts to take risks? Do the following Risk Exercise below to develop your risk-taking ability.

Risk Exercise

1) *Be vulnerable and honest* with yourself and admit: "This feels like a bit of a risk because…"

2) *Do a risk-analysis* that includes: "If then…then what".
   This helps you to think ahead of the possible scenarios, the cues at the tip of the iceberg you need to pay attention to, how you would pivot, and the outcome you are focused on achieving. Outline these thoughts below.
   - Possible scenarios:
   - Cues at the tip of the iceberg I'd watch for:
   - How I would pivot:
   - Outcome I want:

3) *Explore and test your hypothesis.*
   If this still feels like a big risk, do a small pilot/pivot before making a huge change. Remember: Scientists even test their hypothesis before they make a conclusion. Think about how you can do a test, pilot or small pivot.

Now that you have read through all the descriptions of the 15 Characteristics of an Intuitive Leader, rate yourself below so you know where you are doing well, and where you need to improve. Do this on a regular basis to keep yourself conscious. Just a word of caution: Be careful to not use this evaluation to beat yourself up! Should you notice any area that needs improvement, just ask yourself, "How might I improve this characteristic?" Then, listen to what our intuition has to say and then, just do it, as Nike says!

15 Characteristics of an Intuitive Leader:
(Rate yourself from 1-5. 1-never; 2-sometimes; 3-average; 4-often; 5-always)

___**I-**Introspective

___**N-**Non-Judgmental

___**T-**Truthful

___**U-**Undaunted

___**I-**Instinctive

___**T-**Trusting

___**I-**Integrated

___**V-**Visionary

___**E-**Engaging

___**L-**Love

___**E-**Exploratory

___**A-**Accountability

___**D-**Determined

___**E-**Essence

___**R-**Risk-taking

_____ Total Score

Summary of your Intuitive Leadership Evaluation

Excellent Score: 75-61:
You are operating at level 5 consciousness most of the time! Congratulations! You have overcome your fears and negative beliefs about yourself so that you are now only listening to your wisdom—your intuition. In addition, because you are Intuitively Aligned—you have the guts to speak up and do something about it! This is making you an Intuitive Leader, both in your personal and professional life, who is not focused on being right or being liked. You are focused on achieving your vision, values, and goals —and the risks it might take to get there!

Very Good Score: 60-44:
You often are operating in alignment with your intuition and being an Intuitive Leader most of the time. But sometimes you don't follow through with what your gut knows. This is because you sometimes focus on your attachments to the outcome; verses what it is you want to create. Go back to Level 4 consciousness: Detachment and work on what you need to do to let go so you can surrender to your intuition in all situations, especially when you sense a perceived risk or criticism. Work on what you want to create and then use the S.T.O.P. Technique in the moments that matter so that you can get to Intuitive Alignment. You are there most of the time!

Average Score: 45-29:
You are self-aware and catch yourself most of the time so that you are not leading with your fears of the outcome. But there are still times your mind wants you to over-analyze the potential risks and outcomes so you can play it safe. In addition, while you often catch yourself, you still find yourself wanting to react in a fight or flight manner too often. Spend some time doing 'The Work' to clear your fears and negative beliefs that make you wonder if you are enough.

Below Average Score: 30-14:
You are allowing your fears, negative beliefs, and attachments to the outcome to drive your decisions most of the time. This means you are putting your fears, negative beliefs and attachments before the vision, values, and goals. This is what is keeping you from being the Intuitive Leader you are meant to be: You are thinking about how things will affect you! Do 'The Work' to let go of your fears, negative beliefs, and

attachments. This will help you to put your intuition front and center, so it can guide you to achieve your vision, values, and goals.

<ins>Needs a lot of work: 13-0:</ins>
You are still showing up as someone who is trying hard to please your boss or anyone else you give your power and authority away to because you think they control your safety, security, love and need to belong. This means you are focused more outward than inward on your intuition. Because you are spending a lot of time trying to please others and to be enough; you are not spending your energy on thinking about how to achieve your vision, values, and goals—with the help of your intuition. Spend time doing 'The Work' to uncover your negative beliefs and fears that are driving your desire to please others and be validated by them. This will help you break free of your fear and rise to higher levels of consciousness.

In summary, when you practice the 15 Characteristics of an Intuitive Leader, you can be assured you have the skills and approach to be effective in reaching your vision, values, and goals in both your personal and professional life. The 15 Characteristics act as a benchmark for you to hold yourself accountable on how you are showing up, at work and home. Are you being a leader in your life? Or are you giving your power away to someone you have deemed as your authority? Likely if you are not showing up as a leader, it is because you believe someone has the power to control an outcome you are still attached to, such as: Money, status, love or a sense of belonging.

But, as you practice the skills and characteristics throughout the book, you will, however, reach new levels of consciousness that will help you to detach from these illusions that others have power of you. As you realize you don't have to give your power away, you begin to tether to your intuition and make better choices for yourself in each moment. This includes the 7 areas of your life: Vocational, Financial, Physical, Mental, Emotional, Spiritual and in your Relationships. As you can see, awakening to higher levels of consciousness will help you to be intuitive and a leader when you have internalized these skills and traits. Becoming an Intuitive Leader is not precedented on a title or position of power. It is the position you take in your own life when you begin to trust the authority within. As you have learned in the book, becoming an Intuitive Leader is an inside-out job.

For example, when you notice cues at the tip of the iceberg and practice the 15 Characteristics of an Intuitive Leader, you will know when to step into situations and be an advocate for your vision, values, and goals—both at work and home. Remember: If you react to any situation or person, it is because you have made it about your fears and insecurities. This means you are back in the lower levels of consciousness, once again. That's when you will see drama all around you—because you are not conscious of your problems or how your intuition is giving you a gut-alert to pay attention. As a result of your unconsciousness, the cues will get bigger and louder, until you decide to step into them to resolve them, with the help of your intuition.

However, the more you apply these characteristics and skills you've learned in the book, at work and home, the more they will become integrated as a part of you. Then, when others resist or criticize you and your ideas—you will not take it personally, nor will you react. You know that when you take it personally, you have given your power away to others again; instead of trusting your intuition, which is your authority within.

However, if you should get a punch in your gut that makes you feel fear and insecurity again, you can be sure that you are experiencing: The Velcro Effect. As you learned in the book: Just notice that you are in a sticky situation because at some unconscious level you are feeling 'not enough'. If you have a hard time shaking your feelings of fear and insecurity, then get on the elevator and press level one: The Basement Floor of Unconsciousness. This will allow you to do 'The Work' to clear any unconscious fears and negative beliefs that are telling you, "You are not enough!"—deserving enough, capable enough, or lovable enough. Know that believing that you are not enough is a lie—as all things are possible with the help of your intuition.

As you work to awaken to higher levels of consciousness, there will still be times when you feel a little more 'stickier', or a bit more 'witchier', or somewhat more 'wimpier' than you normally would feel. It might be something simple such as: a bad night's rest or you have been so busy lately you've stopped your 5 Practices to Elevate your Consciousness. If that is the case, just start back up with your practices again and soon you will be back to your higher level of consciousness: Intuitive Alignment.

These unprecedented times call for Intuitive Leaders now more than ever! Every one of us has an area of influence where we can be an Intuitive Leader. You might be a teacher, a parent, a caregiver, or a community volunteer—or maybe you are that leader at work. Practicing the 15 Characteristics of an Intuitive Leader will help you to make a positive difference.

As you step into your situation, whatever it is, don't question yourself when others have not yet come to your level of Intuitive Alignment—simply smile! As you explain your intuitive knowing in a clear, calm, and confident way, you will point out how your gut, heart, head—and intuition—have gathered information in this way:

- *Your gut alerted you* to something that needs attention and you clearly name it.
- *Your heart aligned you* to what you value and what to create—and you can clearly, and calmly, name that direction you are aiming to achieve.
- *Your head assimilated the possibilities* to meet your vision, values, and goals—while you can remain open-minded to hear others, and your intuition.
- And *your intuition guided you*—giving you that "a-ha" knowing—a heightened awareness that put all the pieces of the puzzle together to help you understand why that decision would be best, given the circumstances. And you can confidently articulate that!

As a result of your ability to quiet your chattering mind, you now know the difference between that fearful ego's voice, and the wisdom of your intuition. Now that you can discern between the two, you have the wisdom to know the truth and the guts to do something about it. As you are certain and confident in yourself in this way, others will feel your inner knowing. This will help them to believe the information you are presenting, so they can get up to speed with your increased Gut Intelligence™ (GQ).

Above all, remember: Becoming an Intuitive Leader is an inside-out job! The more you are Intuitively Aligned, the less you are affected by other's reactions and the outcomes that may occur. This is because you are connected to your intuition, instead of looking outside of yourself for validation that you are enough.

You know when you have done 'The Work' of detaching from the illusion that you can get safety, security, love and belonging from any specific person or thing—when you can allow others to resist you; and you can simply observe that resistance with pure curiosity. You know this is true because you have experienced what happens when you are open, trusting, and allowing your intuition to guide you—it's like magic! They no longer have the power to create the resistance because you step into the synchronicity happening. You can do this because you are not attached. You are open, trusting, and allowing of your intuition to guide you and supply you with all you need. This is what makes manifesting the life you want more effortless. You are manifesting because you broke free from your fear that was getting in the way of Intuitive Alignment.

Now, you no longer give away your power to someone or something else. This is because you have developed a strong internal locus of control. By turning inward to your intuition for guidance, instead of looking outward for safety, security, love and belonging—you become the authority and creator in your life. And the more aligned you are with your intuition, the more you are this way in all areas of your life—at home and work.

Even if speaking your truth risks a reaction from others—you will be true to yourself.

Finally, remember: Things may not always unfold as you thought they would or when you thought they might. But that's okay! You will be a leader who is in the present moment—ready to handle whatever comes your way because you will ask your intuition your curious question,

"How might we handle this?"

And, you will know when your intuition is speaking to you because you will get that 'a-ha' knowing, a heightened awareness that tells you exactly what to do or say to be effective now. This will help you break through your fear so you can become the effective Intuitive Leader you were meant to be! And remember: Being an effective Intuitive Leader is not a matter of title—it's a matter of influence. And you will have a powerful influence on everyone around you because you have increased your Gut Intelligence™ (GQ).

No matter what your circumstances might be, you can awaken to higher levels of consciousness. All you must do is quiet your chattering mind, break free from your fear, and choose to listen to your intuition to guide you to the answers you need. But remember: Your intuition is not like a Fairy-Godmother or Genie-in-a-bottle that you can call on whenever you have a wish. Your intuition is a relationship you develop with yourself by doing the practices, developing the skills, and doing 'The Work' in the 5 Levels of Consciousness outlined in this book—on a regular basis. When you do 'The Work', you create a new neuropathway, called the gut-brain axis, and develop increased Gut Intelligence™ (GQ). This will allow you to make effective decisions, in the moments that matter, so you can effectively align your decisions to your vision, values, and goals.

It's time to awaken to this authority within that wants to help you break free from your fear—so you can become the Intuitive Leader you were meant to be! There has never been a more uncertain time where our Gut Intelligence™ (GQ) has been needed. But when you take the time to awaken to your intuition, you will eventually know what path is exactly right for you!

Be patient while you embrace each level of consciousness in the present moment. You will awaken to the awareness you need to know at that time so you can be the Intuitive Leader who is clear, calm, and confident in your decisions. And, as you face a few bumps in the road, and twists that may require a pivot, always remember: This or something better is coming your way! You've got this—with the help of your intuition!

REFERENCE INDEX

[1] Australian Spinal Research Foundation, ,"The Three Brains: Why Your Head, Heart and Gut Sometimes Conflict,"
https://spinalresearch.com.au/three-brains-head-heart-gut-sometimes-conflict, July 26, 2016

[2] John Hopkins Medicine, "The Brain-Gut Connection,"
https://www.hopkinsmedicine.org/health/healthy_aging/healthy_body/the-brain-gut-connection

[3] MaClean, Dr. Paul, "Triune Brain Theory,"
http://www.thebrainbox.org.uk/triune_brain_theory/triune_brain_theory.html

[4] Hadhazy, Adam, "Think Twice: How the Gut's "Second Brain" Influences Mood and Well-Being," Scientific American,
https://www.scientficamerican.com/article/gut-second-brain/ February 12, 2020

[5] Turner, Kelly, Ph.D., "The Science Behind Intuition-Why You Should Trust Your Gut",
https://www.psychologytoday.com/blog/radical-remission/201405/the-science-behind-intuition

[6] Lewis, Tanya, "How Men's Brains Are Wired Differently than Women's," Scientific American,
https://www.scientificamerican.com/article/how-mens-brains-are-wired-differently-than-women/ December 2, 2013

[7] Harvard Business Review, "Research: Women Score Higher Than Men in Most Leadership Skills", https://hbr.org/2019/06/research-women-score-higher-than-men-in-most-leadership-skills

[8] Tannen, Deborah, "The Power of Talk: Who Gets Heard and Why", Harvard Business Review, https://hbr.org/1995/09/the-power-of-talk-who-gets-heard-and-why October 1995 issue

[9] Thompson Ph.D, Jeff, "Is Nonverbal Communication a Numbers Game?" Psychology Today. https://www.psychologytoday.com/blog/beyond-words/201109/is-nonverbal-communication-numbers-game/ September 30, 2011

[10] Massachusetts General Hospital, "Depression on the Rise During COIVD-19: Resources for Patients and Their Families", June 25, 2020, https://www.massgeneral.org/news/coronavirus/depression-on-the-rise-during-covid-19

[11] Scientific American, "Intuition May Reveal Where Expertise Resides in the Brain", http://www.scientificamerican.com/article/intuition-may-reveal-where-expertise-resides-in-the-brain May 1, 2015

[12] The Washington Post, "Harvard neuroscientist: Meditation not only reduces stress, here's how it changes your brain", Brigid Schulte, May 26, 2015   https://www.washingtonpost.com/news/inspired-life/wp/2015/05/26/harvard-neuroscientist-meditation-not-only-reduces-stress-it-literally-changes-your-brain/

Susan K. Wehrley is an Executive Coach and author of the following 10 books:

AWAKEN

THE YOGI EXECUTIVE

GUT INTELLIGENCE: ALIGN

GUT INTELLIGENCE

EGO AT WORK

IGNITE THE PLAN

PAUSE

THE PERSONAL LEADERSHIP PUZZLE

THE POWER TO BELIEVE

THE SECRET TO "I AM"

You can learn more about Susan K. Wehrley, her books, and services at:

www.BIZremedies.com

Email: Susan@BIZremedies.com

Phone: 414-581-0449